Mental Toughness:

21 Mornings Program

Transform Your Life into a Miracle with Morning Routines That Make a Shift in Your Mind to Stop Procrastinating, Increase Productivity, and Achieve Goals and Success

Cameron Stone

complete information. No warranties of any kind are declared or implied. Readers acknowledge that the author is not engaging in the rendering of legal, financial, medical or professional advice. The content within this book has been derived from various sources. Please consult a licensed professional before attempting any techniques outlined in this book.

By reading this document, the reader agrees that under no circumstances is the author responsible for any losses, direct or indirect, which are incurred as a result of the use of information contained within this document, including, but not limited to, — errors, omissions, or inaccuracies.

Table of Contents

Introduction

Have you ever had a mental breakdown in the middle of the day after dropping something on the floor or leaving something in the house and just wondered what is wrong with you? Well then you have come to the right place. If you are constantly stressed out and feel like you aren't moving forward in life no matter how hard you try, maybe it's time to step back. Think about the adjustments you need to make so that you can get to where you want to be.

Adjustments might not necessarily be some big change in your life that has to happen right away. More than likely, the small things will make the changes over time. Small changes make bigger differences down the road because you are going to be forming new habits and moving forward into a more organized state of planning. Creating change in your life is more of a mental transformation than anything else because even though it does take physical changes to make a difference, all the processes start in our mind.

If you don't exactly understand what's going on in your life, that's okay. You need to identify what causes your stress and anxiety. Take a look at every aspect of your day. When do you feel the most stressed or the most out of control during your day? Is it when you have too many things to finish? Maybe it's when you're at work and feel like you're not in the right state of mind to be working. Maybe you're having a hard time focusing on the things that need to be done. Whatever it is, by building mental toughness, you can easily calm your mind and channel your energies to create a calmer environment for yourself. You'll be able to take in more information and have a more organized thought process even when you have a lot on your plate.

The first question you have to ask yourself is "What is mental toughness?" The obvious answer is this: mental toughness is your ability to force yourself to do the things that you don't necessarily want to do and to push yourself to complete your daily activities and improve on the stressed-out portions of your life. However, it goes a lot deeper than that. Mental toughness comes down to the different aspects of your life and how you manage them in order to better yourself and live happily. Life is hard. There are days when things are just not easy. You go to work, and you do your job. Then you have to go home to cook dinner, do house chores, and so on and so forth. There are always a lot of things that you have to deal with in your life. You have to prepare for every day, and it's not easy. If life were easy, you wouldn't be here reading this book, trying to figure out how to get ahead. This book will teach you how to manage and deal with some of your super stressors and anxiety triggers. There will be times when you won't be prepared, and we'll address that as well later on.

"However, there will come a time in nearly everyone's life when no amount of practice or preparation can ready you for a challenge or obstacle you will face. And you can bet if you are on the road to greatness, you will face challenges or obstacles at some point. This is when many give up, quit trying, or are derailed totally. After all, it's in these times that goals begin to be questioned—maybe even start to seem 'impossible' or out of reach" (Sly, 2018). This is the part where you have to toughen up and push through all the problems and struggles that you are experiencing. Having mental toughness isn't going to be an easy task. If it were, everyone would always be successful, and there wouldn't be any levels to compete for. Mental toughness takes a considerable amount of effort and perseverance. If it were easy to learn how to have mental toughness, then everyone would be able to do it. But it's a talent that not a lot of people have acquired in their life.

Mental toughness is your ability to overcome doubts. It's your ability to handle stress when things become overwhelming. It also deals with time management. You have to organize your life around the things that need to be done to achieve your personal goals. Whatever point in life you are at right now, think about where you want to be. Do you want to have a lake house one day? Do you want to be the CEO of your own company and calling the shots? These big dreams and goals are achievable if you set your mind to them. It's not easy, and no, it isn't going to happen overnight. You have to believe in yourself and be ready to be different. Hone the skills needed to form a better life.

Mental toughness incorporates a lot of different aspects of your life. It involves getting organized and figuring out the best setup for yourself. However, you aren't just organizing your life. You are also organizing your mind. When there is too much going on around you, things get flustered. You have to center yourself and make your mind less chaotic. You may not be able to control the outside aspects of the world, but you do have the power to decide how you're going to let those things affect you and your mental state.

When you begin to feel that overwhelming sensation, the urge to give up increases, and it feels like a relief to sit down and just blow things off when you're tired. But how are you going to feel later when there are just so many things to do, plus the ones that you decided not to do previously? You have to decide what you want to spend your energy on and what isn't worth the time.

There is going to be a lot of unseen circumstances that arise, and with the right mental training and willingness to set yourself up on a mental toughness standard, you will be able to overcome any obstacle and handle that stress with more ease than you normally would. Improve your self-worth and self-confidence by forming a positive mentality that things will work out for you because you know that they will.

A part of building up your mental fortitude is also having confidence in yourself and being able to stand up for yourself even when people are trying to tear you down. You have to be able to say that you're not going to tolerate someone telling you that you aren't good enough. A better life starts from within yourself, and you have the power to decide what you're willing to keep tolerating from yourself and other people. The fact of the matter is that in order to have mental toughness, you have to start with yourself. You have to be responsible for the choices and decisions that you are going to make when it comes to your future. If you want to create a better life for yourself, you'll have to learn to demand more out of yourself and accept what you can't change about others in your life.

Maybe you have come here to learn how to be a

more effective leader to your team at work or even how to encourage your fellow coworkers to push through their limitations and be better. Leading a team involves being more mentally prepared than is typically necessary. You have a lot more on your plate than a regular worker. You have to know how to manage people as well as their time while they are working on their assignments. You don't want to have to be micromanaging your entire team, but you know that the work they do will reflect on your leadership style and capabilities. It's not as easy as commanding people around, because the value of their work is being recorded on your shoulders, which is another stressor that you are going to have to overcome on the way to feeling less overwhelmed and more prepared to handle everyday as it comes.

So ask yourself why you're here. What has brought you to this book? Are you working yourself over the edge? Does it seem like you have more things to get done in a day than possible? Maybe you aren't feeling satisfied with the way you are planning your future. Whatever your reason for searching out help, this book is here to get your life organized. It will help you get back on track and stress less about the different things you deal with regularly. It is time to dream bigger, do more, and be happier.

Chapter 1: Finding Your Passion

In this chapter, we will be talking about where to start and the assessments you need to make in order to get things going in the correct direction. Finding your passion is all about enjoying your life and the way that you're living. You will discover how to set goals that are achievable for you and how to feel successful and productive by getting things done and not procrastinating.

Following your dreams isn't always easy, especially if you don't know what your dreams are. In elementary school, they ask us what we want to be when we grow up, and of course, at such a young age, being a firefighter or a superhero seemed like the best possible answer. But what if we ask ourselves that now? Whatever age you are, there is always a bigger goal and a bigger dream out there that you are striving to achieve. We set goals that we believe in, which is why some people have a hard time setting bigger goals and plans for themselves. Think about it like this: if there is nothing stopping you, not money or family or anything preventing this from happening, what would you do with your life?

Would you start your own business? Would you live on the beach in a mansion and never work another day in your life? Maybe you would prefer to travel the world and see all the places you thought you'd never go. That's the dream. That is your forever goal, and it's achievable if you believe in yourself and have patience with yourself.

When you consider what you are passionate about, you might find yourself thinking about things that aren't necessarily profitable, and while your goal to make money and have the life you want is important, you have to find a way to get there. Are you passionate about animals or music? Maybe you wish you could just read books all day. Finding ways to incorporate the things you enjoy and that make you feel more alive and happy into your everyday life is going to have a positive impact on the way you begin your day and how you go about handling the stress of the work to come. Having a piece of your passion in your work will make it so that you don't hate what you are doing, even if it does involve change and perseverance.

A big part of living a happy life is finding time to do the things you enjoy the most. When you are constantly running around and trying to accomplish everything in a short amount of time, it's easy to neglect doing the things you love. Make an effort to take time for yourself. Take a break from all the hard work you've done.

By making time for yourself, you are showing yourself that you are important and that you deserve to be happy even when times are tough. You want to keep up that positive energy as much as possible because it will help to make you feel more secure in yourself and in your ability to get things done. When you have a lot of things to do, pushing aside things that are fun is easy. It makes you feel like you have to get just one more thing done, but in reality, it's causing you more stress because you are not giving yourself time to relax and calm down from all your stressors of the day.

Doing Things You Like

We often get so busy that we forget to enjoy our lives. We are always rushing around and in a constant state of "What do I have to do now?" Make it one of your daily goals to do something you enjoy, whether it is just for ten minutes or an hour. It will help you focus on your day and get things done so that you can enjoy the things that make you happy. When life tends to get stressful and we have more and more that we need to accomplish, we push stuff we enjoy to the side in order to get everything else done. The problem with this is that as we keep pushing things aside and not doing the things we enjoy, we tend to sink further and further into a depressive state. This makes us feel more stressed and more anxious about the different things we have going on in our lives.

It's important to take a step back and think about what you actually enjoy doing. More than likely, you work to make money and pay bills, but does your job bring you joy? Probably not. Most people work their jobs day in and day out because money is a necessary means of survival, but you can't let your life be consumed by that alone. Finding your passion might not come easily, but it should be something that brings you absolute joy, something that you couldn't imagine your life without. Do you love animals more than anything in the world? Maybe you have a passion for hiking and your goal is to climb Mt. Everest. It might not come to you right away, or it might not be something so obvious, but take a look around at the different aspects of your life and ask yourself, "What do I love doing or being a part of?"

There is usually one thing that drives you and makes you want to get up every day and get things done, but there are also the little things that you can enjoy in the process of reaching your bigger dream. You can also find something new that you enjoy, and this might motivate you to accomplish your weekly goals so that you can go out and enjoy yourself. Some people enjoy doing artistic crafts to calm down and relax after a stressful day while others prefer to throw axes at full speed across a room to get their daily frustrations out. Either way, there are plenty of things you can do to find something you enjoy.

Once you find the things you like to do, it's important to make time for them. You can't always set a schedule for fun, but if you're not getting around to do the things you enjoy, then you aren't really doing yourself any good. The practice of "all work and no play" will stress you out eventually, so don't let your bigger goals get in the way of your making time to be happy right now. It's an important balance that you will learn over time, and you will develop a better understanding of this balance throughout this book.

Doing the things you like to do naturally relieves some of the stress, whether it is for a few minutes or a few hours. Just taking a break from all the stressors that you have can affect that way you feel for the rest of the day. Creating new hobbies and different activities, such as going to the movies, or maybe even taking a nap from time to time will also help you to calm down from the extreme pace that you are trying to keep up with.

When you allow your stress level to get too high, it can send you into a spiral of things that seem wrong when they really aren't. We will discuss later how to have better control of those worries when they arise, but if you allow yourself to take a breath and enjoy your life, you'll automatically feel more relaxed. Rushing through your life in order to get things done isn't going to help you achieve your goals any faster and, in turn, might actually end up slowing you down as your stress increases and you stop enjoying your life.

You may notice that when you are starting to feel down about the events in your life that not only do you lack interest in doing things, but you lose interest in doing things you used to enjoy.

Finding a passion that spurs you forward is challenging, but it should be something that brings you joy no matter the situation. Take, for example, the owner of a cat cafe. It's not something that people would have originally put together, because fur in drinks doesn't sound like a wonderful time. But people across the country now are flocking to cafes like this to enjoy their love for coffee and cats.

The idea behind this was that sometimes you just need a break, so why not combine a passion for coffee, which is already a profitable business, with a passion for cats? Mark Twain was a famous writer that loved writing, made a considerable profit from it, and cemented his place in history. He was quoted as saying: "Find a job you enjoy doing, and you'll never work a day in your life." If you take that into consideration, finding your passion needs to be at the top of the list in order to find a lifetime of happiness. While it might take a try or two to really discover what you like or enjoy, never give up on what you want to do or who you want to be before you get there.

Set New Goals

Have a big goal that excites you. Maybe it's going on vacation or getting a new car or climbing a mountain. Whatever it is, make sure it thrills you. Let that be your motivation to move forward in the morning and keep everything going. Having big dreams and plans will inspire you to continue toward that goal. If you want to become a writer, practice writing every day. If you want to become a vet, get up and go to school until you get there. The fact of the matter is that long-term goals and dreams are not going to be easy to achieve. If they were, then they wouldn't be on your long-term goal list. Long-term goals take time, hard work, and dedication in order to be accomplished.

Developing yourself into someone with positive habits will help you live a better life. Habits like waking up early and making your bed will get you started in the right direction so that you can go out and crush your goals. Why do we set goals? This is the future! The only way to get motivated is to motivate yourself. Set some new goals and make a plan that will get you there.

Goals need to be measurable, though. You can't just write "I want to own a lake house" as a goal because that isn't something you can measure. Instead, you have to set it up in different steps, such as putting $100 away into a savings account every month. That's measurable. You can see the money going into the account, and you can set a goal for how long you need to do this in order to pay for your home.

Another example is wanting to be promoted. It's not something that just happens. You make it happen. Set up different sets of goals. Plan to stay after work once in a while and make sure you are caught up on everything. Show initiative by setting a goal to be at work ten minutes early every day and have a cup of coffee ready to go.

Think of yes or no when you set goals. Did I arrive to work ten minutes early? Yes. Did I put my $100 into my savings this month? Yes. Don't set goals that aren't realistic. If you only make $450 every two weeks, you aren't going to be able to put $400 into your savings account on every paycheck. You can have stretch goals, but make sure they are still obtainable.

A stretch goal is set to push your further. It is a goal that is just a little bit out of your reach. While your mission is to reach your initial personal goal, once you get there, push a little further by setting your stretch goal. For example, instead of saving $100, make it $150 instead. If you put your money into the account for the month and you have another $75 on your next paycheck, put it in the account as well, and then you will have reached not only your initial goal but also your stretch goal.

You can have short-term goals as well. Maybe you want to do something like climbing the mountain, or maybe you want to have $2,000 saved up by the end of two months. Whatever your goal is, you can achieve it with the right strategy.

Don't let your big goals overshadow your small ones either. You can work toward multiple goals at once, and you should. You are your own motivation because even though you have people encouraging you and telling you, "You're doing great," if you don't want it to happen, you won't make it happen.

"If a step you're doing isn't working, think of something else you could try that still moves you forward, even a tiny bit. If you're struggling, ask people you know for their ideas on what you could do. They may help you see a different way. Thinking about different ways of reaching our goals makes it more likely we'll be successful" (Action for Happiness, 2017). Sometimes we need to let other people help us to see a better path. When you get stuck in a rut with seemingly no way out, other people looking in can often see a different number of solutions or tactics that can get you back to where you need to be.

It's okay to let people help you during your goal setting as well because maybe they can give you advice on how to start on some of your harder goals while staying motivated and keeping yourself on the right track for success. When you have people behind you that are giving you support and encouraging you to do your best, you end up having more courage to work harder and more quickly toward your goal. Having an emotional support system and friends that are behind you, while not essential, does encourage improvement over time because it creates a need for accountability.

Setting goals also come with a lot of personal development skills. You're not going to wake up one day and suddenly be super organized and prepared to give a speech about success if you haven't prepared yourself for that. You'll learn more and more about how your brain operates. You will learn the best ways for you to work through different obstacles and get over large hurdles. You will eventually develop your routine and be able to look at your list of goals and know where to start for you to work in the most effective way.

No matter what age, the first goal in the morning that anyone should set is to get up on time and make the bed. This will begin your day on the right foot. Why make the bed? Because making the bed is like getting everything together—putting the sheets on straight and folding the comforter over, setting all those pillows back on top. This morning routine is not a lot, but it's a habit that will make you accountable to yourself.

You don't have to know every one of your goals right away. Things change, and through this process of development, you might very well change, too. Whatever your goal is now, go after it. If in a few months or a few years, that goal may change, and you may suddenly have a whole new dream. Write it down and plan it out. You can do whatever you set your mind to as long as you make the plan to do it.

When it comes to the workplace and setting new goals, you may find this to be more of a challenge, especially because not only are you dealing with the demand from the top of the work chain coming down, you also have standards that you are responsible for achieving on a regular basis for the company. When setting goals for your team, you're encouraged to try and make it fun for them, because it is more motivating to achieve the goals that get you excited than the ones you're just commanded to work towards. People like having a healthy competition, and that's a great way to keep spirits up in the workplace, especially if it has been difficult getting company standards up. It's also beneficial to sit down with each member of the team one-on-one and make personal goals for each person. By breaking down the bigger goals into smaller ones, just as you would do for your personal life, it makes the whole process seem more manageable and helps your workers feel like the road to success isn't as daunting as it may look.

You might also want to have your team members assign themselves different goals for the week outside of what you have decided to work on together. Much like yourself, they are trying to be better, and by making them pick their own goals and create stretch goals for themselves, it makes them more responsible in the sense that not only would they be letting you down but they would also be letting themselves down if they fail to meet the goal they set for themselves.

Chapter 2: Hard Reset

- While we are not computers, our brains oftentimes will act like them. Think about when you're too tired and you have a million things on your mind. It feels like you're moving in slow motion, right? It's because your brain is trying to process too much information all at once. You have too many tabs open on the computer, and it's causing you to process information slower and with less clarity. You can only keep up with so many things at once, so when you try to skip a few steps and get all your to-dos done at once, you're going to end up missing a few things along the way. Not to mention, if you keep starting new goals or activities, you might eventually crash your system into a panic-attack-styled meltdown.

Doing a hard reset on your life can bring about a few challenges. It can be an emotional or physical change that might be needed. You might not realize how out of whack things have become. You might try setting your new life up but still have a hard time. The purpose of the hard reset, though, is to let everything go and start afresh. Don't keep any negative energy. Don't keep old items that you no longer use. You need to start over.

I think one of the best ways to start a reset is to buy a new calendar and notebook. Having a clean slate for your notes is what will keep you organized. You don't want to be scribbling notes everywhere. Try to use sticky notes or only a certain part of a page of a notebook if you need to jot things down. Seeing a bunch of scribbled nonsense on a page is going to confuse you. It's easy to lose track of something if it's written in the corner of a page where you aren't looking.

When you crowd a page with notes and scribbles, it can cause anxiety to build because you don't know if everything is done or if there is something left to do. Keep things organized. Focus on making a simple list that you can cross items off when you complete them.

Think of going to bed like "sleep mode" on a computer. It's not completely shut down, but it's giving the computer a rest from all the background apps and activities you've been using it for. Your brain is operating on the same functions. Bad dreams have been linked to stressful days because your anxieties and worries are carried over to the dream world, causing restless sleep. If you have had a particularly stressful day or week, you can always try different techniques such as meditation or positive reinforced thoughts to help you relax at night.

When you don't get enough rest at night or have a high-stress level acting on you, it can become overwhelming in your head and make you anxious and depressed. When you get too overwhelmed with the things going on in your life, you're more than likely to have a panic attack at some point or another. Ignoring your body's cry for help is going to stress you out further, and this can cause you to slip into a depressed state.

You can make changes in your everyday life that are small but impactful in the way that you get things done. You don't have to change everything you do immediately. In fact, it isn't recommended that you do so because it could cause you more stress if you try to go in and change everything all at once. Decide on one or two things that you want to start working on changing and start there. If you try to do too much at once, you will end up frustrated and failing at all of them. Focus only on one situation at a time. When you have complete control over that one aspect of your life, you can then work on changing another one. Don't do too much at the beginning, or else you'll end up discouraging yourself from continuing.

In this chapter, we are going to discuss the ways

to take control of your life and emotions. You will learn how to reset your mind when things become a little too chaotic in your brain. Using better planning and making action steps for you to follow, you will be able to get a better handle on the task you need to accomplish. Your emotional well-being will improve as well.

Doing a hard reset on your life can be a bit challenging because you have to be willing to let go of all the worries and stressors that you have at the moment. When your brain is trying to focus on too many things at once, it causes you to fail and, much like a computer, crash. Doing a hard reset is all about reorganizing and putting together a better plan in order to help you accomplish more of your to-do list as well as reach your biggest goals. A big part of doing this hard mental reset, though, is being willing to hold yourself accountable for the action plans you put in place. Even once you have cleared your mind and determined your goals, you still need to execute the tasks needed and be willing to force yourself to do them.

Let's Make a List

The first step to prioritizing is knowing what has to be done. The initial step for anyone who needs to get his or her life back together is to make a list of everything, big and small, that needs to be accomplished. Find a medium that works for you. Some people live their entire lives on their phones. If that's you, there are tons of list apps available. You can also just use the notepad app on your phone. If you prefer a pen and paper, then keep a small notebook, and make your list there. The whole point is to always have the list with you. Make sure that no matter what medium you choose, you have it with you whenever you need it.

I also recommend having multiple lists. It will help you keep your ideas in one place but separated into different sections. I personally separate my list into daily, weekly, and then monthly. Obviously, the daily list consists of things that I need to get done that day. They must get crossed off the list by the time I go to sleep that night. My weekly list typically consists of things that, while not immediately needed, do have to get done. Usually, this is meal prep for the week and laundry for the following week. The weekly list might also have appointments scheduled and items that need to be picked up on a certain date.

The monthly list contains more goals than to-dos. My monthly list contains items such as putting $100 into savings or getting the spare room decorated. These are bigger task and goals that could very well take more than a week to get done, which is why I put them on the monthly list and don't cross them off until they are actually completed.

The objective is to not overwhelm yourself by putting too many things on one list. You want to keep things spread out in order to maintain control of everything going on. A list of to-dos shouldn't have any more than ten tasks because that's when things start to become too much to handle. If you have more than ten things that absolutely have to be done that day, set a very firm schedule for yourself and stick to it as closely as possible so that you're not running around in circles.

When making a to-do list, think of the most important things first. The items at the top of your list should be of high priority, and those at the bottom should be things that just need to be completed. By putting the most important items at the top of your list, you are more likely to get them done first, and then you don't have to worry about accomplishing them later in the day. We will talk about this more in the time management section. Working on your most important tasks in the morning will reduce stress. Since those things are already out of the way, you don't have to worry about running out of time to get them done by the end of the day.

You also want to break your bigger task down into smaller ones. For instance, if you have a research paper that needs to be done in a few weeks, put it on your monthly to-do list, but you should also break it down to smaller portions for your weeks and days. To do this, for example, you can create an outline for the paper, research and notate ideas, and research chapters 1–3 deeper. By breaking down your bigger task into smaller ones, you take some of the pressure of having to do this long project all at once. Instead, the small steps will help the whole picture come together at the end.

Tasks and goals are similar in a way that they are somewhat measurable. Like the example above, be specific with the things you need to do. Research chapters 1 to 3 and then develop an outline for your paper. Each task should be specific to what you want to get done. While it may not be a numerical measurement, it's still a way to hold yourself accountable to achieving that specific goal.

I like color coordinating my steps because it makes it easier for me to find the things I am looking for. I keep all my big goals in black pen with a yellow highlighter running through them. This way, I can easily recognize their importance and know this is the bigger picture. This goal right here is why I wake up every morning and go do my job even when I'm exhausted. I write in a blue pen for pieces of my monthly goals that I want to get accomplished that week, and I write in a black pen for all my daily task and goals.

However you decide to go about getting yourself organized, make sure it works for you. Developing your goals is step 1, and you've accomplished that step. You have your dreams and goals all jotted down with space for more when they develop; now develop your list of plans and steps to achieve those goals. It's not an overnight process, because life isn't simple like that. It takes time and patience and belief in yourself that you can make it happen. Hold yourself accountable for maintaining that list. Check your items off, big or small, and add new things when you need to. Continue the process and do not become stagnant on planning your future.

Get Up and Get Going

When the alarm goes off, it's time to get up. Hitting the snooze button (while tempting) is going to start your day off bad. Getting up on time is the beginning of a successful day. I used to think that this wasn't really all that important, but it makes a huge difference because it's the beginning of your personal development and how you want to change. By beginning your day earlier in the morning, it helps you develop a more steady routine. You also have more time to get things accomplished. Nobody really enjoys waking up early, but if it is going to make your life easier, wouldn't you want to do it? Help yourself out by setting your alarm and getting up when it goes off. You're beginning to hold yourself accountable for getting everything done, including getting up on time in the morning.

If you have ever laid in bed, staring at the ceiling, wondering what the point in getting up is, you're not alone. So let me tell you the point. You get up to accomplish your dreams. You go to work to accomplish your dreams. You make everything happen to get you somewhere else.

Getting up is the first step to improving on your day. If you don't get up, how are you going to get anything accomplished? The trick to get motivated is to remind yourself why you are getting up to do your work. What inspires you to get things done and accomplish your work? Are you working toward one of your bigger goals? Are you trying to accomplish a task that you have been working on for a long time? Whatever it is, reminding yourself why you are getting up is going to help you stay on the track of getting it done.

It's tempting to oversleep on weekends, but those are the days when it is important to get up early. You have to accomplish as many tasks you can during those days when you aren't working. Planning your weekend errands and tasks is essential to get the most out of your day. A lot of places close early on Sunday. You have to make the most out of the time you have on Saturday and the limited time you have on Sunday. Plan to do your main tasks on Saturday and start as early as you can manage. You can always start early and then take a nap later in the afternoon, but you might run out of time to get things done if you decide to sleep in late.

Self-doubt might sneak in on you and make you feel like things aren't going to work out, but you have to shove those thoughts aside. Get up, make your bed, and start your day. Open your notebook where you have been writing all your notes and plans in, along with your multiple to-do lists. Decide what you are going to accomplish today.

Better planning is going to take you a lot further than you think. Most of the time, you have to work backward to achieve your goals. See the end result you're trying to achieve. When you want to bake a new recipe for dinner, you find out everything you need and then you go get those ingredients, right? You do that because you already know the end results. You get what you need, and you complete all those steps because you are able to visualize and form the reality that you will be eating that new recipe and it will be delicious.

Start with what you want to achieve. When you wake up in the morning and you're staring at the ceiling, what do you want? You want to be successful, but only you can do that for yourself. Get up and start acting on your plans. Holding yourself accountable for the actions and plans that you make is a part of personal development that is often forgotten about. You're always thinking about the things you want to change about yourself and how you'd do it, but you have to make that change.

For example, if you want to become more athletic and fit, but you have never worked out a day in your life, what is the first step? It's going to the gym. You go even when you're tired and when it's raining and when you have eight other things to do because you are accountable for yourself. You made the decision that you wanted to be fit, and that is your goal. You may or may not have people cheering you on and encouraging you, but only you are responsible for yourself. You wake up in the morning and get out of bed for yourself. You get dressed and go to work to make your money. Make goals and dreams for yourself and then make your plan to accomplish them.

People are going to tell you to wait. They will say good things will come and you will be successful if you are patient. However, patience has seldom brought anyone success. When I decided I wanted to a writer, it was because I had a passion for writing. I dreamed of being a writer, but I was terrible at grammar.

My family would tell me that it would come with time and that I would develop a larger vocabulary and understand more about writing styles and formats. However, that answer wasn't good enough for my dream. So I researched and developed a plan to get me to where I wanted to be as a writer. I learned from books and from other writers, and I developed a skill set on my own because I had a dream and I made it happen.

When you wake up in the morning and visualize your dream, breathe it in   like it is your life. Decide that it is the reason you get up every day. What are you holding yourself accountable for? Are you going be the next CEO because you took the extra steps and you figured out how to get to the next level? Are you going to climb that mountain and become famous for a new world record?

You are accountable for your dreams and your goals. No one can get in your way as long as you don't let them. When you wake up in the morning and you get out of bed and start your day, your first thought should be "I'm doing this because I deserve to make my dream happen. I am going to make my dream happen."

The amount of effort that you put in is proportional to the amount self-improvement that you get back. The first step of waking up and getting started is always the hardest part because beginning on something that will make a big change in your life can be frightening and deterring, especially if you're still unsure of where you want to start. Fear is the biggest deterrent when it comes to achieving goals because people are often afraid of the unknown. If you find yourself afraid to move into these new process or change what you do because you don't know the outcomes, you can overcome those fears by reminding yourself that it's okay if it doesn't work. The first few times you do something, it may not be successful, but you just have to keep putting forth the effort into making that first step work. Once you pass the first step, everything else will seem less scary.

Time Management

There are only so many hours in a day, and trying to accomplish everything that needs to be done can take a toll on anyone. Oftentimes, we forget the small tasks, and they accumulate until they become overwhelming. It's best not to overwork yourself. You shouldn't have more than ten things on your daily to-do list. The problem with having a long to-do list is that even if the items are easy to accomplish, it can cause your brain to send a distress signal, and you might become anxious without even realizing it.

While we plan for everything to go smoothly, that isn't always going to happen. When planning for big dreams and big goals, it's important to keep in mind that things are going to go wrong, but you can get back on track with good time management skills.

When you look at everything that needs to be done, that list can seem exponentially long when in reality most of the tasks can probably be done simultaneously. If you're in need of groceries but also have to get loads of laundry done, you can start a load and then go to the store. By the time you return, the laundry can be moved over, and another load can be started. You have now finished two tasks at the same time.

Think about how long things normally take. Next to each item on your to-do list, put the approximate time you think you will be able to complete it. Don't overbook yourself, though. Your day isn't a race, and you shouldn't try to make it one. Time management helps prevent stress because you have a plan in place and you know how long things are going to take to get done.

You can apply time management not only to your everyday tasks but also to your life goals. If you want to live comfortably by the age of forty, then set a plan and a timetable for when you need to reach your financial goals in life. A lot of people forget about financial planning, and it is one of the largest stressors that people have. No matter what age you are starting at, planning out a retirement strategy for the future will help relieve a lot of stress later on in your life.

Begin a savings account specifically for your retirement or for a vacation you want to do when you are older and plan to put about 5% of your paycheck into that account when you get paid. While the money might not grow rapidly, it will help you in the long run and reduce your concerns in the future as well.

You can also organize the tasks on your list

according to the amount of time it would take for you to do them if you prefer to do it that way. If you know that something is going to take a long time to finish, such as getting your car looked at, then schedule that at the beginning of your day. This way, you can go ahead and get that task out of your way completely, and you can move on to the items that will take less time to accomplish or that you can do simultaneously.

If you work on the most important task during the earliest part of your day, it will help you feel motivated to accomplish the rest, because the biggest task has already been completed. When the weight is lifted off you, you feel like you can breathe a little easier and get more things accomplished during the remainder of the day.

Another big part of time management is sticking to when things need to be done. If you said that you were going to finish doing the dishes by 3:00 p.m., then you need to get them done. It comes back to holding yourself accountable for your actions. If you say you are going to do it, then hold yourself to that standard and get it done. It's easy enough to push the small stuff to the side when you are tired of working on another task, but it forms a positive connection in your brain that you are responsible.

Always hold yourself accountable for the task that you set.

"Routines help us to trust the process and not focus on the outcome" (Fader, 2018). Sometimes looking too far into the future can cause you too much anxiety. Instead of focusing on everything to come, focus on the now and what you are doing at the current moment because the rest will follow. Your problems aren't just going to disappear, and despite how much you try to plan or schedule, there will be times when things just don't work out at all as you planned. Prepare to take those tasks in strides and focus on the things you can control and the things you can accomplish in the here and now.

When things seem to be overwhelming and you begin to get that lost feeling despite having a schedule and a plan in place, it's time to take a break. You have to realize that in order to be successful, you will have to accept the changes and problems that are going to be thrown at you.

Time management is going to take you further in life. You need to plan how to effectively fit all your tasks in your schedule in order to get more things done in a short amount of time. Make it a habit to regularly list all the things you need to do and make a schedule of when you have to work on them and for how long. This way, you will develop a routine, and you will know what works most effectively for you. While it seems time-consuming and unnecessary to schedule your tasks, this will make you more productive. You will also develop a memory of how long something would take to do. Your schedule will be ten times easier to manage because you'll have a head start on the things that can be finished that day.

When it comes to time management on a team, it can sometimes be challenging to keep everyone on task. Assigning different tasks to different people is the most effective strategy to get things accomplished. Look at all the different tasks you are being held accountable for, and assign different aspects to different workers.

As a leader, you will be assigned multiple things at once, whether it be just for your team or an entire office. Similar to how you made a list to get your personal items together, you can also make several different list in order to help your team members accomplish all the tasks they have. Sometimes making personalized lists can help workers accomplish more in a short period of time.

For example, if you are responsible for getting ten credit cards per day, then you could assign two cards per worker in order to achieve the total needed. This keeps them focused on a task while also helping your team to succeed. Making lists for team management can also help you determine where certain people are falling short or may need your help. If they are unable to get something done in the time frame you would typically expect, then they may need some follow up guidance to get them back to your standard of success.

Time management is not just the amount of time it takes to accomplish certain tasks, but also planning out a schedule to make sure everyone gets their fair share of work. Being in charge of a group is stressful, because you have quite a few more task that you are in charge of. You may find yourself lacking time when it comes to getting schedules put out and assignments recorded, which is why it's good to have that time set aside for yourself to accomplish the task you know will take you more time. This way, you won't feel rushed to get things accomplished during a time crunch when your coworkers need assistance. If you need to make a work schedule, plan to sit down for an hour without interruption and get it knocked out before you have people asking you a hundred different questions all at once. If you know that you have to get status reports sent to your boss and you need a quiet place to do it, you need to set aside the time to go somewhere where you won't be interrupted. While it does take more planning and some extra steps along the way, the path to being a leader and staying in charge isn't one you should expect to come easily.

Chapter 3: Journaling

Journaling is a great way to organize your thoughts and get your plans on paper. A journal is where you can write down your notes and new ideas. Having a journal that you update every day will also help you to track your progress and mark things off your to-do list as you work toward your goals.

Keeping a record of all your different tasks, plans, and schedules in one place will help you stay on track and make sure that you don't lose track of anything. Keeping everything together also helps you track the progress that you are making.

Journaling can seem like a waste of time, especially at first. However, you will eventually begin to notice its benefits. The trouble of having to remember all the things that you need to do will be lifted off you as they are all listed in your journal.

You may also have these big dreams that you're chasing after. Your journal will remind you why you are going after that dream. Dedicate two or three pages at the front of your journal to your goals and dreams so that you can immediately turn to these pages and be reminded of what you're working for. Plus, if you have a few spare pages, you can add new goals in there as   well as you develop as a person and become more of who you want to be.

You might want to keep a specific page dedicated to your achievements as well. You can look back on what you have already accomplished, and this will make you feel good. You have reached these goals, which means you can succeed in your other dreams and goals as well.

Your journal should be used for self-expression and getting your emotions out when they start to build up. It's important to remember that it doesn't need to be perfect. It can be filled with scribbles and jotted ideas as long as it stays organized enough for you to understand them. You may have days when you have pages of information you need to write down, or you may have nothing to say at all and all you do is draw a smiley face on a line next to the date. Break your journal in and make it your own in order to use it more efficiently.

Writing something down daily will help you develop the positive habit of keeping track of different tasks, but it also allows you the freedom of clearing your mind from the stress you dealt with during the day. While your day might not have been overly busy or what you consider to be stressful by definition, it's easy for small things to build up. If you have already taken the time to write them down and make a plan for either how you plan to deal with those emotions or ways to manage the tasks, then you won't have to worry about that coming back down on your shoulders. If you do start to worry about the same things again or deal with the same or similar stressor, you can flip to that page in your journal to remind yourself what you can do to calm down and bring yourself back to having peace of mind.

If you do decide to use your journal as a way to get emotions out from the day, I would suggest either dedicating a fresh page to it so that it doesn't crowd your list or other jotted notes, or you can write it on the bottom of the page away from your list. However you go about organizing your journal is completely up to you, but in order for it to be useful you do need to keep it organized and legible so that you know what needs to be accomplished when in order not to stress yourself out. Journaling is supposed to be a way for you to be able to relax and relieve yourself from the stress from the day. However, if you do not feel that writing emotions down is going to be beneficial for you, then there isn't a need to force yourself to do it. The process of finding what works for you is all you need to focus on when it comes to writing down information.

Your journal doesn't have to be a fancy notebook. It can be a spiral notebook from a dollar store or a notepad that you can easily toss in your bag. You can even use your cell phone if you find that more convenient. As long as you have your journal with you and use it whenever needed, then that's all that matters.

One Page Change

Wanting something to change isn't going to make it change. I'm sure at some point in your life you have said, "I wish I had a million dollars." But so does everyone else. Wishing for something isn't going to make it happen. What's going to make it happen is hard work and dedication. You can't just work on a long-term goal for a few days; you have to keep working for it over and over until it practically doesn't feel like work anymore because you are so used to it.

If you are seeking change in your life, then do something. You can't just throw an acorn on the ground and expect it to grow. You'd have to carefully plant it in the ground and water it daily until it sprouts. Let it have sun, give it more water, and be patient while your acorn grows into a tree. Yes, this process is going to take years, but when you have a beautiful full-grown tree in the yard, you will be proud of it and what you've accomplished.

There might be struggles along the way as you try to change yourself for the better, and write them down in your journal. You have to keep track of what you're feeling as well as what you are doing. This will help you handle yourself better in the future.

Journaling is a good way to keep everything together in one place. It might not be in perfect order, but by keeping your thoughts and feelings in one place, along with your to-do list and schedules, you'll be able to focus more on getting things done. You will also become less disorganized.

As we talk about journaling and planning a successful future, it can easily become overwhelming when things don't go as planned. Don't get discouraged though. Life is hard, and that's something to know in the back of your mind every day. It's hard, and things might not go according to plan, but that's why you make a new plan. Don't expect to see a change right away. Developing new habits is a process, and it isn't going to happen right away just because you want it to.

When you think about journaling, the first thought that comes to mind is typically someone writing pages about their emotions and things that happened during the day. This is a very large misconception. You can jot down notes, make a bullet-point list, draw diagram plans for the future—whatever makes you comfortable and happy with your journal and keeps you in good mental health.

Some people like to write down their notes and to-do lists using different colors. This helps them get their thoughts organized. By using colored pens, you can easily tell what goes where.

Starting on a fresh page every day is important because it creates a blank slate for you. Even if you don't end up using the entire page, keeping your daily list separated will keep you organized and focused on that day only. When you try to merge your previous day's list into today's list, it can become confusing. By creating a new one on a new piece of paper, you're eliminating any confusion, and you can focus solely on what you've written down for today.

Let's say you didn't complete your list on Friday. Instead of flipping the page over or scribbling another list on Friday's page, just add the missed items to your Saturday list and cross them off there. I recommend doing your monthly list first and then writing your weekly list on the next page before doing the daily list. Having it in calendar order will keep you organized on the time frames. You can date your pages in advance so that you know where to put your new to-do lists.

You might want to cut out a small calendar and post it in your notebook to mark specific dates that you have events to attend to. You can highlight, draw arrows, and make symbols, whatever you need to do to make a legible key for you to follow. This will keep you organized and better prepared for the day.

You won't see any changes overnight; however, when the month is up and you flip back through your journal, you will be able to see how much you've actually accomplished during the previous weeks. You will realize that you are progressively getting more and more things done with your improved momentum. You are developing mental toughness and forming positive habits.

Although you mainly use your journal for writing down your to-do lists and goal planning, it's also a great place to get out anything else that's on your mind. During the process of change, there can be a lot of doubts, and you can start to feel down when things aren't going exactly as planned. If you write these worries down on the days that you have them, you will be able to see how, after a period of time, you were able to overcome and handle those situations.

Writing down how you feel and all the negative emotions that you experience while going through this process will help you get your frustrations out. As you work on your journal and how you organize your lists, you're going to be able to see the time frame on how quickly you get things accomplished. This is going to help you set realistic goals as well for the future, because you will have a better understanding of how well you get certain task accomplished or when you need to start working on projects. A lot of planning is experimental at first until you develop the right flow for yourself. So don't worry yourself over change not happening quickly or not seeing any habits forming. Allow yourself the benefit of a few months for forming good habits. Your journal will allow you to see the places you excel and those where you need to focus in order to be more successful for yourself.

Self-Esteem and Self-Doubt

A big part of change is the ability to have a positive mindset. You're stressed and depressed and when you reach the end of your rope, you don't exactly know what to do. Most of the time, you just go blank and have a small meltdown before beginning to climb back up that rope again and get back to what you were doing before.

First things first—get off the rope. You are just stressing yourself out more and more by trying to get up that rope to accomplish your personal goals. That rope is going straight up, and while straight up is the quickest way to the top, it isn't the most effective. You have to take the stairs when it comes to progression. Maybe you're able to climb the rope on certain things, like getting your to-do list done or making sure you make the bed every day. If you can, that's great. Do it. For more complicated things that are not easily achieved, such as getting a promotion at work or starting your own business, turn to the stairs of growth.

Each stair has its own set of instructions to help you get to the next one. You have a new problem to overcome on each stair, and with each one that you climb, you will get closer and closer to your goal. Some stairs may be harder to climb than others, and that's normal. It can cause a lot of frustration and discouragement, and that's what brings us back to mindset.

The thought of "I can't" or "Maybe tomorrow" has to stop. Procrastination is the enemy of success because it just makes you believe you can continue to put things off. For example, when you're on stair 4 and it seems impossible to get to stair 5, you start to say, "I'll try it tomorrow" or "It can wait until Friday." It can't wait, though. You have to correct that train of thought. You have to keep trying to get to that next step because no one is going to do it for you. The longer you procrastinate, the farther from your goal you will be.

The worst part of self-doubt and low self-esteem is that it isn't a passing feeling typically. You have to take a moment to embrace that feeling and drill down to the source. What is it you are struggling with? Is it your work life or your personal life? Are you even sure why you're upset? Try to focus on tangible things to get yourself to calm back down. If you get too wrapped up in your head, you will find yourself starting to fall down the rabbit hole of fear and frustration, which is what you are trying to avoid the most. While fear is a natural enemy of progress, you can't let it stand in your way of success. Your mind might already be trying to go on its way down a negative path of uncertainty, and you have to force yourself to stop and turn back around to face your goals. Procrastination is just a way to delay the process of facing the uncertainty you feel and stops you from making any real progress towards your better self. You can be nervous and you can feel doubtful about the next steps because that's a normal reaction, but you just can't let it stop you from continuing your plans to better thinking.

The best way to start off the new process is to change your way of thinking. You have to let the negativity go. Begin to think positively and focus your attention on the things you can control and the things you want to get accomplished. Now that you have thought about the things you enjoy doing and have written down a few measurable goals that you want to accomplish, it's time to start acting on those things. Thinking positively about what you want to do and get accomplished will really help motivate you to get it done. Positive thoughts help to convince your brain that you like what you are doing. It's the same idea that if you just keep smiling, things will feel better. You will start to be happier just because you are smiling even if the situation seems bleak.

The purpose of setting goals is to help you stay on track in life. It keeps you motivated and excited about things that are coming. Keeping up your motivation and excitement for life helps prevent depression and anxiety from consuming you when things don't go according to your life plan. Anxiety happens when you have too much going on in your head and don't know how to handle it, and depression occurs when you start to fail in doing your tasks.

Anxiety and depression are working in sync in your head, which is why staying focused and knowing what you need to get done for the day is important. While the anxiety-controlled portion of your brain is sending signals that you have too much going on, the depression part is telling you that you are incapable of doing all these things in the time that they need to be done. This is where your newly set goals come into play. By knowing that you only need to achieve a few things that day, you will be more focused on the task at hand, and you will be more capable of controlling the thoughts inside your head. Don't try to do too much. If you overbook your schedule and begin to feel overwhelmed, it opens that door for self-doubt and worries to come in and start to lower your self-esteem.

Depression is an emergency brake for success because it's creating an abundance of self-doubt all at once. Depression causes you to feel like you are incapable of getting anything done and there is no point in even trying to get things done because you won't succeed. That emotion creates the thought pattern that you can't do something or that you won't be successful in that role. You have to realize what is happening, and shut that negative voice down. While this thought process is demotivating, it is important to force yourself to continue being extra vigilant when it comes to getting things done and revisiting your goals. Remind yourself of the reasons why you keep going. Stay positive.

Depression and anxiety work together to cause extreme amounts of stress, hindering your motivation to accomplish your goals. While anxiety screams at you about all the things you need to get done, depression tells you just to sit down and not do anything. You will feel lost.

When you begin to doubt that you are moving in the correct direction, it's good to review the things you know for sure. Below are three things to think when you begin to doubt yourself:

1. Have I done everything in my power?

2. What is actually bothering me?

3. What can I do now?

"Have I done everything in my power?" This question is the first one to ask yourself because when you doubt what you have done, make sure there is actually a reason. For example, when you are preparing for an interview and you have self-doubts, give yourself a rundown of everything that you've done. Did you wear a nice outfit? Did you introduce yourself? Did you shake hands? Did you research the company? By asking yourself these questions, you will either realize that you didn't do everything you could have or figure out that, yes, in fact, you've done everything you could have possibly done in your situation. If you didn't do everything in your power, don't let that destroy you. At this point, it is over. Let that anxiety wash away and take the problem with it. Next time, you will do better because you know better, and that's okay.

"What is actually bothering me?" Anxiety and depression create a compound effect. The compound effect is when all the little things that are bothering you on the surface start to build up.

Some bigger issues are thrown, along with some unnecessary concerns, and suddenly, you have the compound effect hitting you full force with more worries than necessary. The best way to handle the compound effect is to stop what you're doing and breathe. Bring out your journal. Write down all the things that seem to be bothering you and think about what you're seeing. The things you have written down, are these actual problems? Is there anything on that list that you can change? Yes? Change it. No? Let it go.

It's easier said than done, and that's normal. However, it is also a part of mental toughness to convince your brain that it just isn't important anymore. It will come easier with time, but for the current moment, take a deep breath. Think about the things you can change and those you can't and then come up with your solutions. Oftentimes, you may find that everything on your list is already done and that you are worrying about things you cannot change.

Lastly, "What can I do now?" Questions 1 and 2 answer that for you most of the time, but if you are still uncertain of what you can do, the best thing to do is to stop and breathe. Your mind is working too fast, and you're not able to actually keep up with everything you are trying to process. Let everything slow down and come to a stop for a moment. By continuing to keep up with everything, you're just forcing your brain to work on more things all at once. Give yourself a ten-minute break to process and complete all the thought patterns that you need to. Once your mind has settled, you will find that you can think more clearly. Refocus on what needs to be done. Shut down the negative thoughts and doubt that you had previously.

Self-doubt and anxiety often sneak up on you. Typically, self-doubt is something that builds up over time instead of something that you feel right away. That's why it's important to recognize the signs before you are hit by a tidal wave of emotion. The first sign you'll see is when you start not to want to complete a task that you typically do all the time. When you are used to doing something and you suddenly just start to feel like you don't want to do it anymore or someone else does it better, that's an immediate red flag that you are starting to feel that self-doubt.

Another red flag is when you don't feel like you can accomplish anything. It's not that you couldn't; you just have no desire to complete anything because you don't feel like it's all that worth it. Another sign is being hyper-aware of everything that you have to do and trying to figure out how to accomplish them all in one day.

When these signs start to appear, you need to take a step back and realize that you're starting to get a little overwhelmed. This is when you'll want to take a few deep breaths and focus only on what you can control at that moment. Don't worry about anything else. Just remind yourself that you are worthy of your goals, that you are successful at what you do, and that as long as you keep doing your best work, it will all be okay.

When you feel like you are starting to experience an anxiety attack or beginning to feel depressed, there are a few things you can do that should help you calm down. Exercising is a big factor when it comes to mental health. Getting out and stimulating your brain keeps the endorphins that create happiness. "Develop a routine so that you're physically active most days of the week. Exercise is a powerful stress reducer. It may improve your mood and help you stay healthy. Start out slowly and gradually increase the amount and intensity of your activities" (Sparks, 2018).

You also want to make sleep a priority on your list. Go to bed at a reasonable hour and get up on time as well. There is no need to be tired all the time. Getting eight hours of sleep is vital to the way we function and how we feel emotionally through the day. If you don't get enough sleep, you are likely to feel irritable and less focused on the items that you need to get done. Be well rested and prepared for your day. You don't, however, want to sleep too much of your day away. Sleeping too many hours can affect you negatively. It will make you feel more tired than you should, not to mention that it leaves you less time in the day to get things done.

Eating healthier will also affect your mood. It seems harmless to swing by McDonald's or Burger King on the way home, but by continuing to eat junk food, you're more likely to feel down and not up to finishing out your day. While there are no proven results, healthier foods, like fruits and vegetables, have been linked to anxiety reduction in the average person.

Whenever you're facing a problem, self-doubt and fear may come into play. While some problems are easier than others to face, you will have to be prepared to talk yourself through the different challenges in order to overcome those fears and doubts. It's easy enough to get sucked into the hole of despair as things get harder, but as long as you continue to push through and remind yourself about all the positive things you have going on, then you will be able to get through the hard parts.

If you manage to get caught in a hole where you struggle to get out, going back and looking over your goals can help to excite you and motivate you back into the game. You can also talk to coworkers or friends about what you are hoping to achieve in the future; this will help you develop some accountability in the future. Getting stuck doesn't mean you should give up, though. There might be a week when you fall off the wagon on your practices, and that's okay. Just get back on track and recenter yourself, focusing on what you want to accomplish and why you want to accomplish it.

Self-esteem in the workplace fluctuates constantly. When team members begin to feel like they aren't doing a correct job or are having trouble fulfilling the goals and tasks that they were assigned, it can make them feel like they aren't doing a good enough job and lower their overall self-esteem. While you may not have control over the way that someone else feels, you can control the way you handle the situation. Offer help to your coworkers when you see them becoming overly stressed out. A negative work environment can and will affect everyone there, even if it stems from just one individual.

Embracing Vulnerability

Vulnerability is a topic that is hard to talk about for some people, even though it ought to be something that we embrace regularly. Our vulnerability is what makes us human and gives us insight into the way that people act and how they go about dealing with things. "Employees want to work with a human, not a robot, and most people are excited to talk about their personal lives and emotions, either good or bad. Build connections with co-workers through real, honest conversations. Having open, non-judgmental conversations fosters an environment of cohesiveness and teamwork where people feel they can share issues and ideas, both personal and professional, in a safe atmosphere." (Morgan, 2017)

People spend so much time at their workplace that it becomes like a second home to them in some ways. So being able to express themselves and the emotions they have during their work day is essential to their mental wellbeing.

You may be asking how this ties into the idea of mental toughness, since we are talking about vulnerability, and the answer is simple: relief. Change is already difficult and while you are in the process of change and forcing yourself to become more resilient to work and stress during your average day, you are going to need a break from the constant pressure. People are going to want to support you while you work on bettering yourself and your future, and if you are working with a team that needs help with focus, talking about your ups and downs during the process could lead to some breakthroughs.

When we think about vulnerability, we typically think about women throwing their emotions around and a lot of crying, but it isn't always like that. Being able to express your emotions and concerns in the work space opens up the line of communication so that people are better able to understand what one another are going through and perhaps give advice or simply be there for support if asked.

Marina Plata, writer for Psychology Today, talked about what her first job as a psychological clinic assistant taught her: "I learned about teamwork, responsibility, and assertive communication. Three components which I consider being crucial to any work environment. I learned how to voice my concerns and opinions, and I learned how to place boundaries between my personal and professional life – something that a lot of therapists struggle with."

To put that in simpler terms, even people that are trained to deal with other's emotions can struggle to keep it all under control. If you focus in on the three things she learned, you'll see assertive communication on the list. Communication is the key to any successful relationship, whether it be personal or professional, and that's why vulnerability is important. If you are unable to communicate how you are feeling in the workplace, then there will be a divide between how people see you and react to you in terms of guidance.

Chapter 4: Accountability

We have done a lot of talking about accountability and holding yourself to a standard on your own, but what does that really mean and what purpose is it serving? When you make a promise to someone, you follow through on that promise because that person is counting on you. You know that they are entrusting you to do what you said you would do.

In this case, you're building that reputation with yourself. While you tell yourself that you are going to do your tasks and work toward your goals, there is no one to answer to but yourself. If you hold yourself to that promise and prove that you are accountable to yourself, it makes getting tasks done much easier. It also promotes a positive internal relationship with yourself.

It can be really hard to hold yourself accountable, not because you don't want to succeed but because if you aren't used to forcing yourself to keep up with something, having the willpower might not come naturally to you. A great way to begin working on your willpower and ability to hold yourself accountable is to start with something small, such as making your bed every day. Being accountable for actions like that will help you to form habits that are going to keep you motivated throughout your life while keeping you organized and on a good life path.

By keeping yourself accountable for making your bed, you start forming the positive habit of organizing things as you begin your day. Starting off with simple tasks will make it easy for you. It can be challenging to jump from not doing a task to suddenly doing a huge one. Ease yourself into the process and start with a small task to enable a smooth transition.

It's important that you build a strong reputation within yourself. If you cannot count on yourself to get something accomplished, why would anyone else be able to? You have to prove to yourself that you are responsible enough before you are able to show anyone else what you are capable of doing. You can't expect to become a leader if you keep failing in your tasks.

By being accountable for the actions you take toward reaching your goals, you end up pushing self-doubt to the side and improving your self-worth in the process. The more you follow through on something that you told yourself to do, the more you will develop self-worth. When you do what you need to do, positive things will happen.

Holding yourself accountable isn't always

positive. This is something to keep in mind when you are unable to finish certain tasks or if you decide to put something off for another few days. Failure only happens when you don't improve on something. So yes, you messed up and didn't complete the list of things you set out to do, but holding yourself accountable and saying, "I messed up, but tomorrow I will do better," that's still a positive outcome. Whenever you mess up on a task or are feeling demotivated to follow through on your dreams, remind yourself that you are worth it, that your dreams matter.

There will be days when you just have too much to do and will feel very overwhelmed. If things don't get accomplished, accept it, move on, and try again tomorrow. Be responsible for yourself and follow through on the promises and tasks that you have assigned to yourself because no one is standing there over your shoulder cheering you on. It's up to you. You can do it!

Never forget that while you are accountable for you, as a leader or manager, you are also accountable for the actions of others if they are unable to complete their tasks as well. So while you do have to maintain a level of professionalism and can't command workers to get it done, showing team members how to be accountable for their work loads and the importance behind it will allow the team to work together smoothly while everyone works fairly to get everything accomplished in a timely manner.

Twenty-Four Hours

Break down the hours in a day and use them to your advantage—this is necessary to create a calm life. Set your goals into a schedule and work around problems in the day without freaking out. Granted, most of the time after work, there isn't a lot of daylight left and you have a lot of other things you want to accomplish before going to sleep. That's why making your schedule and deciding what you can get done that day is important.

Let's start with a basic breakdown of the day. You sleep for eight hours and work for eight hours, plus you likely have a lunch break for about an hour. That is already seventeen hours of your day, which leaves you with seven hours of productivity. Once you're off work, you're tired and stressed from the day, and more than likely, you don't want to get things done. However, you need to pump the breaks on that thought process and reset yourself on a positive track. Mental toughness kicks in when you remind yourself that this was your promise to yourself. You said, "Today, I am going to accomplish this," and so you need to do it.

If you're having a hard time keeping that thought process going, flip through your notebook and remind yourself of everything you have already accomplished and the goal that you are currently working to achieve. This should help you put your mind back on a positive track. Motivate yourself to keep going and push aside that tired feeling.

Let's say your to-do list for today has grocery shopping for the week and meal prep. If you don't already have the supplies for dinner and lunch the next day, it's easy enough to stop by the store on your way home and pick up the ingredients you need in order to get that done. Keep your shopping under an hour, and then when you get home, have time to fix food without being stressed out. It usually takes about an hour to prepare a meal, so you are now left with about five hours in your day.

Keep in mind all the errands that you need to accomplish, and look at them as a whole. Is there anything that you need to get from the store that is close to another store you need to go to? If there is, then it's best to group these to-dos together. That way, you can get them done all at once when you are looking at your list of to-dos. This activity involves setting your schedule as well. When you are making your list for the day, look at everything that needs to be done and group them together ahead of time. This way, you don't have to think about them all later on; instead, you can go ahead and get started on the things you wanted to get accomplished.

With all that being said, you don't want to do too many errands at once, especially on days when you have to work. Your off days are typically the ones when most of your errands are going to be accomplished, especially your high-priority or time-consuming tasks. Get some of the smaller things done, such as making dinner and lunch. Doing a pile of laundry can be accomplished during the week. It can be done after or before work, depending on your schedule.

After a long day at work and now running a few errands, you might begin to run out of steam, which is normal. However, this is where mental toughness needs to come into play. You still have to get things done. This isn't something that is going to go away. You need to eat, and you need to have clean clothes at some point or another. So toughen up and put your adulting pants on. Getting this done will be good motivation for you to keep going even when you are worn out. It also sets a good standard for yourself as you begin to hold yourself more and more accountable for your actions.

Do you want to feel successful and be less stressed out? Do the things that need to be done—that is what is going to make you feel accomplished. It isn't sitting at home and wondering what you are going to have for dinner, no. It's going to the store, fixing a meal, and getting things done. This will reduce your level of anxiety because you will have crossed off two things on your to-do list—buy food, make food, done. Now you have about eight more items you need to check off before the day is over.

Let's just say the next thing on your list is to do laundry. Put one load of laundry in the washer and start it. Look at your list again. Do you need to go to any other stores? Yes? Then go get that errand done now while the clothes are being washed since there is no point in waiting around for something to happen while they cycle through. If you don't have anywhere else to be, then move on to the next thing on your list. Maybe it's vacuuming the bedroom. It only takes a few minutes to get this done but always seems like such a chore when you're tired and not in the mood to be cleaning the house.

A great way to motivate yourself into getting it done, though, is to imagine how much better it will feel when you actually get it done. Five minutes of labor to have fresh carpet to walk on, and you'll have another thing crossed off your to-do list. Granted, it can be a pain to drag the vacuum out and get it plugged up, especially if you have a big room, but this is a part of the program. Convince yourself that you want to do it because you want to live a happier life. Less stress. Less to do. You want to be happy and get things done.

Now that your laundry is done, move it to the dryer and start your process again. Put another load of laundry into the washer and then find the next item on your list that you can cross off. Maybe you need to give your dog a bath. That comes with its own set of challenges, especially if your dog doesn't like baths. But you can do this. Grab your dog up and put him in the bathtub after you have gathered all your supplies. By the time you have finished giving him a bath and getting him dried off, dinner is probably ready and can be taken out.

You can eat and clean up your dishes, and when everything is done, more than likely, your laundry is done too. One of the biggest issues when it comes to procrastination is folding the laundry after it comes out of the dryer. It can be time-consuming, and while it may seem easy to just pull clothes out of the basket when you need them, you're better off hanging them and folding them while they are warm.

You want to be your best self, and having wrinkled clothes and not looking professional isn't going to make you feel good about yourself. Take the extra time to hang your clothes up and put them away. You'll feel better about it in the long run. Have those items out of the way, and don't let them sit in a basket blocking your floor space where you just vacuumed.

The idea here isn't to shove everything into one day and get it all done but rather to look at your schedule and maximize your time. If you can imagine your end results, then you can get there. You can have a nice-smelling dog, prepared lunches, and a clean house; however, it's on you to do them for you. If you're looking for someone to hold your hand and take you through this process, unfortunately, you'll be disappointed.

To be successful and to feel accomplished in yourself, you've got to look past everyone else and all your obstacles. Focus on the future and on the present, because the present is going to get you to the future, and the future is your goal and what you are striving for. Everything in between is just noise. When you feel lost, find your inner voice. Remember what you are going for and focus your energies on accomplishing it all for you and not for anyone else. This is your success story, and you don't need anyone else to help write it but you.

Don't Get Overwhelmed

Another big factor of planning and being prepared is understanding that there are things you have forgotten about and there are things you will think of along the way. It happens, and it is something you need to be prepared for on your way to success. You may have thought of many things during the day, and that's okay. Just put them on the list of things that need to get done. Remember that all you need to achieve is today's list.

It can be overwhelming especially when your to-do list seems long. However, that's why you need to have weekly and monthly to-do lists as well, because not everything has to be done that day. Focus only on what you want to accomplish for today. This will keep your stress level down, and you will be more prepared to handle all your activities. You can easily become anxious if you begin to do too much at all at once.

You can jot down the new things you've thought of, and then later on, you can add them to your weekly or daily list when they come around and need to be completed. Other to-dos are going to come up, and there will be some that you just can't get done on time.   Don't   feel overwhelmed.   Take   a deep breath and just focus on the things you did get accomplished. Remind yourself that you are doing everything you can and you will work through it.

Not every day will be perfect, and while you are working to make a change in your life to reduce stress, you don't want this to become all-consuming. Remember, you want to see a more positive and motivated life. Just because you don't finish everything on your list doesn't make you a failure. Failure only occurs when you don't learn from it and don't make an adjustment or change for the future.

Mental toughness is developed over time through perseverance. Developing new habits is a lot like learning to walk when you're a baby. First, the baby has to crawl. This is your time to make a plan and decide that you are going to stick to it. Decide that this is the time that you are actually going to get your life more organized and make yourself happier and less stressed. Then that baby starts to stand. Standing is when you begin to practice these new habits and start developing the muscle strength to keep up with new thought patterns. You fortify your mind into thinking positively. However, before a baby can walk, they often fall. A lot. Don't let that stress you out. Failure is critical to change. So when you fall and don't get everything done, remember, it's okay to fall as long as   you get back up again.

Being overwhelmed can also lead you straight back to self-doubt. This can cause you unnecessary anxiety when all you really need to do is step back and realize that it's easy enough; you just have to reschedule a few things if there isn't enough time in the day. Mental toughness can be overwhelming in itself because you want to see results right away, which should not be the case. When you start experiencing the signs of anxiety and depression forming in your mind again, go back to the previous chapter and read through it again to help you overcome your insecurity.

Being in charge is going to occasionally get overwhelming, and struggling to keep yourself afloat may seem impossible, but you have to keep reminding yourself that while you're in charge of a group, you do have some backup from your team. Not everything can be assigned to other workers, but there are definitely some task that you can hand off in order to not feel so overwhelmed by the workload. Small things such as filing receipts and organizing materials in the office to keep the space tidy is something everyone can help out with. You can also assign a team leader to help you out by setting up goals or keeping track of goal progress for the day if you have a lot of different things on your plate for the day.

When you begin feeling overwhelmed at work,

taking a few moments to step back and breathe can really help bring you back into the reality of the situation. You might need to reorganize your plans for the day in order to get everything done that's needed, and that reorganization might include you taking a few minutes to yourself to breathe and center your thoughts on the assignments at hand.

When you become overwhelmed at work, it can seem a lot more agonizing because you know that other people are relying on you as well. In order to not let them down, or yourself down, you need to keep everything you're doing in perspective and focus on what you can do in the moment to get your list accomplished.

Reward Yourself

It's nice to put away 3–5 percent of your paycheck every time you get paid. This way, you can reward yourself by getting yourself something you like, or you can save toward a bigger goal in the future.

We talked about future goals earlier in this book, but this is where your expense planning comes in. One of the most stressful aspects of life is money. There never seems to be enough of it even when it feels like you are working all the time. Savings accounts have a hard time being formed when you are constantly spending money on food and supplies that you need. So while it is hard to save money, if you put away 3–5 percent of your paycheck, you will see gradual growth in that account.

You can always put more into the account as well, especially if you are trying to save up for a big goal, like going on vacation or buying yourself an expensive item, such as a new car.

Let's say you make $2,000 in two weeks and you decide to put 5 percent of that into a savings account. That's only $100, which compared to the paycheck isn't a lot. Every little bit counts. If you don't want to put a percentage into the account, then you can always add $5 per paycheck or a different amount when you can.

Money might not be your answer, though. Find a reward that works for you. Maybe you like going to the pool and reading a book after being cooped up in the office all week. So plan a weekend that you can take a few hours to yourself and relax at the pool. Maybe you want to sit down and watch that movie that everyone is talking about but you haven't had enough time to see.

Whatever it is, rewarding yourself is just as important as accomplishing the task. Rewarding yourself tells your brain that you did a good job and that you are working on making a positive change. When you get everything on the list done, celebrate. When you accomplish one of your monthly goals, celebrate. Maybe one of your yearly goals was to reach a target weight loss. If you succeed at that, reward yourself for a job well done.

You're making a change for yourself and not for anyone else. When you are less stressed and worried, you will be more motivated to get things done, and you will feel more accomplished with yourself. You don't have to be 100 percent all the time, but you'll eventually get to that point where knocking off items on your list comes naturally and easily. Reward yourself for your successes but don't punish yourself for failure. Change takes time.

You also want to reward yourself when times are getting tough. Everybody needs a little bit of a push in the right direction. Rewarding yourself for the continuous progress that you make will keep you excited and in the spirit of accomplishing your goals.

Rewards don't have to be extravagant. It can be something as simple as going out and getting some of your favorite chocolate or renting a movie and taking some time to relax instead of worrying about everything else. Whatever you decide to do, let it be something worth doing. Consider it a brief pause in our hectic life. Let things go during the time you're taking a break.

The point of rewarding yourself in the middle of trying to reach your goals is that you need to feel success starting to build. This will move you forward in the direction you want your future to go. You don't have to feel like things have to be completed before you can treat yourself, but don't get carried away. Rewards are for rewarding good behavior and the efforts that you are putting into achieving your goals. You don't want to just treat yourself when you haven't made any progress or accomplishments.

Chapter 5: Twenty-One Days of Change

Twenty-one days don't actually form a habit. The reason for this idea is that by the time you reach that twenty-one-day mark, you are just through with the second stage of forming a habit. There are three stages that make a habit happen (Selk, 2013). First, you have the honeymoon stage, where you are just starting off and everything seems relatively easy. In this stage, you have a very positive outlook on this change. Then you have the second stage called the "fight thru," and that's where you're twenty-one days end. However, if you have reached this point and continue to push through, you're going to make it to the third stage, which is "second nature," where the habit becomes instinctive being it has taken root.

It's that "fight thru" stage that you have to survive, though. In this stage, you begin to doubt your ability to form this habit and be successful in the new development. You're still at the point where slipping into an old habit is easy enough to do. But if you want to change (and you're reading this, so you do), you have to push past those negative thoughts and tell yourself to keep going.

Remind yourself why you have come this far. Look at the goals you have already reached and the ones that you are going for now. Look at your successes and remember that you accomplished them all on your own because you set your mind straight to your goal.

While you are forming a habit, though, there will be a lot of changes that you have to make. Make sure you stick to your plan and make it happen even when you reach the tough parts. You have to be positive and determined. You have to want to make that change. While you're making changes in your life, you will probably see a lot of personal development begin to happen, forming you to become a better version of you.

When it comes to change, I encourage you never to feel like you aren't doing enough. Things will change at a different rate for everyone. Don't be discouraged when you see some people making changes at a quicker pace than you. You have to focus only on what you can control, and that's what you do to form habits in your own life. Developing a new habit can be painfully annoying, especially if you are trying to replace a bad habit with a better one. You need to keep reminding yourself why you are doing this and what you are aiming to achieve in the end.

Goals and habits coexist because you often have to form some good habits in order to reach your goals. You can't just wake up one day with the ability run a marathon or have the skills to be a mathematician; however, you can work toward those goals by focusing your strengths there and making the necessary changes.

If you want to stand out and be a leader, harness your personal talents that will build you up and make you more successful. Habits for personal gain and habits for success go hand in hand. You need to strive to improve your personal and professional life. Don't sit back and let others tell you what to think. Speak up, and if you have a different opinion, then so be it, because you could be the one to start the change around you.

Positive Thinking

Positive thinking, while rather self-explanatory, actually has a lot of power behind it. The same goes with negative thoughts. We have talked about how to redirect your thoughts when you are starting to think negatively. But what is actually happening in your brain when your thoughts turn bad? James Clear, a behavioral psychologist, states, "Negative emotions narrow your mind. . . . The problem is that your brain is still programmed to respond to negative emotions in the same way—by shutting off the outside world and limiting the options you see around you."

The idea here is that once you enter a negative state of mind, you have to fight your way back out. Your brain only processes thoughts one way, and it shuts down every other possible idea that arises. In a negative state, you only focus on the negative and the things going wrong. So when you start to struggle in your tasks, the negative thought process will take over.

Positive thinking takes more mental strength than you may anticipate. It can be challenging to keep a bright and upbeat attitude when things begin to feel overwhelming and out of control. These are the moments when positive thinking matters the most though. If you can keep positivity in a stressful situation and push through those negative thoughts, you will strengthen your mind and build up your capabilities, keeping yourself motivated.

Positive thinking is useful when you are in a stressful situation that is out of your control. Being in this situation can be demotivating since it feels like you are just going up against a brick wall. You have to keep your positive energy up. Keep looking for reasons to smile and be happy. If you let that negativity and bad energy get to you, you're going to end up feeling down. If you start to feel down, you will likely feel less motivated to accomplish anything that you want to do.

Positive thinking and self-talks are great practices even when you feel stuck in a hole. Positive thinking, for obvious reasons, keeps you in a good light. It makes you feel that successful glow inside, and it does have the motivating power to keep you moving forward. Self-talks are also worth doing. Sometimes, talking to yourself is all you need to do in order to make yourself feel better.

Do you remember watching television and the characters would have mental monologues when working out a plan or scheme or when trying to figure out what to say to their parents or crush? Self-talk is practically the same concept. You can use self-talk to keep you motivated. Talking to yourself will help you get through the different things that you are working on. You can also use self-talk when you just need to sort through some confusion in your mind.

When your mind becomes overwhelmed, self-talks can also help you to work through problems that you are having. Sometimes, people will mention talking their problems out with others in order to get the realization of what is causing the problems, but you can always bounce the ideas off yourself as well by talking aloud. When you talk to yourself out loud about a certain situation that is bothering you, your mind processes the thoughts in a different manner because you have to slow down in order to actually say them, giving you time to think. By processing the question in a slower fashion, you can think of different solutions.

Draw a map if it helps, but when you're trying to trace back your anxieties or solve a problem in your head, talking out loud can help you to focus. Self-talk is also a great way to go about clearing your head. Some people talk to the wall; others like to talk to their pets like they understand them. Do whatever helps you to get those thoughts and feelings processed so that you can move past them and onto the other things on your agenda.

What does this mean when it comes to developing new habits? It means positive thinking does not only keep you happy and in the positive light but also keep your mind open to new possibilities. You become open to new dreams and goals because you're not feeling closed off to new ideas.

Maybe you're sitting there, thinking, "I'm pretty positive, but what can I do to increase my positivity?" Well, it comes back to finding your passion. What brings you joy? Find the things that make you happy and that make you want to laugh and smile. These things will promote positive thoughts.

If you start to feel down, try centering yourself. Focus on the things that make you happy. Remember happy things, and you will be able to calm yourself and bring yourself back into a state of happiness and positivity, reopening your mind to other possibilities.

"Happiness is both the precursor to success and the result of it" (Clear, 2018). What does that mean? If you have ever said, "I'll be happy when or if . . ." then you are that precursor. You're pretty much looking for happiness from success, and in turn, happiness comes from success. It makes plenty of sense. You're not going to be satisfied by failure, and it won't be something that keeps you content. You want to be successful and happy.

But on that same note, don't let success be the only reason for your happiness. If you constantly go through life thinking that the only way to be happy is to be successful, then you're going to run into a lot of negative thinking and unrealistic goals that you can't meet. You have to be happy with yourself. Work hard to be the person you want to be to become successful.

Positive thinking is something that has to be practiced as well; it doesn't always come naturally. Whenever a negative thought pops into your head, try to turn it into a positive thought instead. For example, instead of thinking, "I'm not improving," try telling yourself, "I've just got to try again." It comes back to the "baby walking" scenario. You are going to fall a few times, and you can't let that be what dooms you. Having a positive outlook affects your entire well-being and how you view what's going on around you.

"If you tend to have a negative outlook, don't expect to become an optimist overnight. But with practice, eventually, your self-talk will contain less self-criticism and more self-acceptance" (Mayo Clinic Staff, 2017).

If you wake up every day and remind yourself that

change takes time and in time you will change, you will succeed. With every step that we talk about in this book, it all comes down to being patient and resilient. You have to believe in yourself. Stay focused on what you want because it isn't an overnight fix. It could take weeks, months, and even years to reach some of the goals that you are going after. These stepping-stones of accountability and personal improvement are going to help you every day as you get closer to your goals, but achieving change is a goal by itself. You have to work to make change happen in every aspect of your life, whether it be thinking positively or having less self-doubt. You have to develop time management skills. Set new goals and update your to-do list because you will always have new tasks to face every day.

Be Kind to Yourself

Positive thinking is going to take you a long way in terms of getting your mind in the right space, but you also need to be kind to yourself. You need to be aware of how you are feeling mentally and physically. If your mental health is struggling, your physical health may be struggling as well.

Take inventory of your life and your health. "Your mind won't operate efficiently if you're not fueling it with sleep, exercise, and healthy food. But don't make your goal to be thinner or to look good in a bathing suit. Aim for building a healthy body so you can enjoy a healthier, stronger mind." (Moran, 2017)

So much of the time we are in a rush and we are trying to accomplish more things that we can handle, so we grab fast food and keep on moving. When this happens, you're not doing yourself any favors. You're going to feel just as tired and probably be hungrier sooner because of a bad lunch choice. Fast food isn't going to give you the nutrients and energy that you need in order to get you through the day.

The stress you are under can also cause you to struggle with sleeping. If you aren't sleeping properly, you'll be more agitated and unfocused on the job at hand. While you are working on your mental health, your physical health cannot come second. The same thing goes for your team members. If they seem to be lacking in energy and not getting things accomplished, check in on them and see how they are feeling. Have an open line of communication so that when people are struggling, they know that they are able to seek guidance in you.

Just like anything else, you need to be able to take responsibility for your health. You don't get to push it off to the side because you're busy or you're tired. You need to make time to pack food or prepare meals before you eat. If you're able to be more prepared, then that is a stress you won't have to deal with later on. You'll be able to eat healthier and have more energy to make it through the day, leading to improved mental health - all because you decided to take care of and be kind to yourself.

Unlock Your Potential

Going out into the world feeling like you don't know what you're doing is scary, and it's an uncomfortable feeling for anyone at any age. However, that's why you have to get into your groove. Try to unlock your potential and develop skills that you are already good at and already enjoy doing. There are three steps that will help you identify your key traits:

1. Identify what you're really good at.
2. Master your craft.
3. Turn that talent into a passion.

Let's talk about identifying what you're really good at. "Figure out what skills have helped you thrive and what made you stand out from the rest. Are you a physically gifted individual who excels at a certain sport? Or are you the type of person who displays intellectual proficiency in a certain area? The key is to highlight your skills so you have a good grasp of what to focus on" (Fuastino, 2017).

You have to think about what you already like to do and what others tell you that you're good at. That's your starting point. Once you know what to focus on, you can center your efforts there and begin to work harder on developing those specific skills.

Then you have to learn to master your craft, which really just comes down to having a lot of patience and practice. "Investing your time, effort, and energy into developing your talents is vital to achieving your fullest potential" (Fuastino, 2017). Developing your talents is tedious, and you might not always want to work on that, but it comes back to having mental toughness. Endure the process if you want to become the best of the best. If that's not the goal, then what is it you're aiming for?

Don't let the frustration of repetition get to you. The only way to become successful at something is to do it about a hundred thousand times until there is no way that you could mess it up. When it comes to mastering a craft, you have to want it more than anything in the world. You have to be so focused and so determined because, in your heart and mind, you know this is what you want to do with the rest of your life.

Turn your talent into a passion. This is the part where things become difficult. One day, you have mastered your craft, and then the next steps might not be so clear. Once you find your niche, though, possibilities are endless. You can open a store if you have something to sell, or you can write advice on certain things you have learned and perfected over time. You're already good at this; now build on it. Take it from being just a "cool talent" to a passion that you can involve the world in. You want to get other people involved in your craft because that's how passionate you are about it.

A perfect example is watching a YouTube video of people showing off their different pets. They have such enthusiasm. Why is that? Because they love and enjoy every aspect of being pet owners. They love sharing information about different animal species because that is their joy and their passion, and that enthusiasm travels through to you as you learn about them. Now, they probably aren't profiting off their love of animals, but what if you were someone who went to school to study animals specifically and became a specialist? You would be capitalizing on your passion and things you love while also being able to help others and share that passion with people along the way.

Now you might be sitting here, thinking to yourself, "I have multiple things I'm good at and enjoy doing, so how do I know where to go now?" Where do you want to go?

Jenna Kutcher bought a camera off Craigslist and built her entire company around that. She liked taking photos, so she stepped up her game on that specific skill and created an empire around her name. "You also need to release the things that don't ignite your fire. Ask yourself: 'I know I can do this, but is this how my time is best spent?' If the answer is no, that you are not using your skills to their best ability, consider outsourcing or delegating" (Kutcher, 2017).

That right there is the key. You can be good at a lot of things, but harness the perfect one for you. Know that skill inside out even when you are blindfolded, and you can make something out of it. You can be good at things and not be passionate about them. That's normal, and those are the things you have to let go of because they aren't going to do you any good. Even if you work to master one of those crafts, you will never really be satisfied with your life if you have no passion for the things you do. You wouldn't be able to inspire others and show people your worth and your value because you wouldn't be showing them what you love.

Sometimes, you may run into the thought of "What if I am not particularly good at anything?" Then your possibilities are endless. If you are absolutely terrible at playing golf but you love it more than anything in the world, start practicing. Get a coach who has taken the time to master this craft and have them teach you. You might have to work a little bit harder because maybe golf isn't   your natural talent, but loving it will inspire you   and   motivate   you   to work harder. You will be putting your passion further out there and reaching for goals from ground zero. But imagine how incredible it will feel when one day you get to tell someone, "I had no idea what I was doing, but this is where determination got me."

Another thing about harnessing your skills is that you should not be afraid to mess up a few times. Quite honestly, you might start harnessing the wrong skill that you thought you wanted. Once you're in it, you might discover that it isn't something you enjoy. Turn back to your journal and look through your goals. Think about everything involved in getting where you want to be. Going back to the golf example, maybe you thought you wanted to be a professional player one day, but it turns out that competition really isn't something you enjoy doing. However, you might find out that talking to people about golf and teaching them different techniques inspires you instead. That's what you should develop on.

You don't have to stay on the same path forever, but once you find that niche and that real passion inside, don't let that feeling go. Let it be the reason you get up in the morning. Let it inspire you to inspire others and build your success story. If teaching is what inspires you, then you can work as a trainer. You can become a coach,   or you can even work up to own a golf course   yourself because while you might not be about golf competitions anymore, your love for it hasn't changed. You still want to be a part of that environment, and there are a million different ways to capitalize on skill sets outside of just performing that skill. Maybe you aren't a doctor, but you're great at business and want to help people, then maybe opening a hospital is the right for you.

The point is that there is no right or wrong when it comes to harnessing your skill sets. Step 1 is to find your passion and go after it with everything you have. Somewhere along the way, you'll find your passion. Develop your niche there, and the pattern will continue until you find yourself where you didn't expect to be but love being.

Use all your potential to your advantage. Every step of the way, you are going to be learning something new and something important. The best way to take advantage of these new skills is to develop them along the way. Maybe you don't love learning all the terms or the subcategories of your particular niche, but one day, you might want to expand into that category. The head start that you already have will put you miles ahead of people that are just starting out. Working hard and getting ahead is the most challenging part of anything, but the more you want something, the easier it is to achieve it. That's the question to ask yourself   every day: "Is this what I really want to do with   the rest of my life?" If the answer is yes, then keep pushing through even at the annoying, tough, boring, and frustrating moments. Being a success isn't easy, and if it were, everyone would be one.

Be Yourself and Be a Leader

Everyone has a different definition of a leader, and everyone has a different perception of how they think leaders should act. When it comes down to leadership, there are a few traits that tend to stand out. In fact, it has been designed as an acrostic and taught across different schools and ages as well. ASCD, a teaching program, defines leadership as below:

Learn: You have to constantly be learning and adapting to change.

Empower: Let people know they can be successful without fearing failure.

Adapt: Everything is changing; change with it.

Delegate: You cannot do everything; give direction.

Engage: You are not alone as a leader, and other people are there to help.

Reflect: Look at what you did and what you need to change and then repeat.

Serve: Others are working for you, but you also are working for them.

Now that we have defined what leadership stands for, let's delve a little deeper into each category. The *L* in *leaders* stands for "learn," and it might be one of the most important aspects when it comes to leadership. You are going to be constantly learning new things and new information to spread to your team, so it's important that you don't get too hung up on certain elements in life because they could easily change and be obsolete in a few months from now.

The first *E* stands for "empower" which holds a lot of stake in what it takes to be a leader. No one wants to stand around and be told what to do and scolded if they mess up. You want a cohesive work environment, and you want to be able to show your employees that they do not have to worry about failing. "People that are empowered find greater value in the work they are engaged in" (ASCD, 2018). If people enjoy what they do and the people that they do it with, they will be more successful, and they will work harder because they feel that they belong and that they hold value to their team.

The *A* stands for "adapt." As we have talked about before, things are constantly changing. There is no forever in anything anymore. We see a constant change in the development of technology and the way that we are teaching students. We see new ways to create machines or design marketing strategies. Nothing is constant, and as a leader, learning and adapting go together. You need to be prepared so that as things change, you learn new ways to accomplish your goals.

The *D* stands for "delegate." Delegation is something that leaders can often struggle with. No one person can do everything. Especially when you're new to leadership, you might try to take a responsibility because you already know how to do it and it would be easier than having to teach someone if they didn't know how. However, delegating projects to other people means you are counting on them and that they have to be accountable to you and to themselves as well. When you have meetings to attend or other things that need to handle, your hands are free from those other assignments, and you are more prepared to take on the more challenging project.

The second *E* in *leaders* stands for "engage." Engaging your team is so vital when you are in charge. You don't want people to feel like they don't matter or that they are being left out for whatever reason. It also gives them a sense of belonging and shows them that you do care about what they think and have to say on matters. If you work in a company that has shareholders, engaging them can either make or break plans that you may have come up. The people under you want to know that they are in your line of   sight and that while you have a lot going on, you're still taking them into consideration.

The *R* stands for "reflect." Reflection comes at the end of your day. After an event or a meeting, you can reflect on a lot of different things. When you reflect, you can learn from the mistakes you've made. You can figure out how to do something better and then improve your processes for next time when faced with a similar scenario.

And lastly, there is the *S* in *leaders*. The *S* is important to remember when leading because it stands for "serve." If someone in management constantly tells you what to do and makes things difficult but is inaccessible when asked for help, that leader lacks the "serve" part. As a leader, it isn't all delegation. You need to be there for your team as much as they are there for you.

Another important aspect of being a leader is being yourself. There is no need to pretend to be someone different. You got to this leadership role because you earned it. You have the experience and the talent to lead, and other people can see that, so don't try to be anything else but you.

Being yourself is a very important step when it comes to being successful. Everyone has heard the saying at some point or   another that you have to be yourself and not try   to be like other people.

However, it always seems like self-preservation nonsense makes you feel like you do not fit in where you are. The truth is, on the path to becoming a leader, you should stand out and not be like other people.

Being able to stand out from the crowd and show off your skills is what will get you to the top. If you're a cookie-cutter replica of all the other regular people, then what are you going to say when employers ask you what makes you different? Especially when you are younger, you want to fit in with everyone around. Although some of the anxiety fades away when you are older, you still want to feel like you are a part of the group.

Don't let being the same as everyone else be your downfall. Go the extra mile and pick up different techniques and strategies. Try different experiences. Push yourself forward in life, and you will have the acceptance and respect of your other coworkers.

Sometimes being yourself can be a challenge because you have to be able to separate personal and professional life when it comes to business. However, that doesn't mean you can't be friendly and you can't have good relationships with your coworkers and subordinates. If your team trusts you and puts their faith in you when you give them instruction, then you have done your job.

Being yourself will also help you face a lot of problems as a leader. If you think like differently, you will probably come up with a hundred scenarios and solutions that might work in the workplace. Think differently and process information in a different way. If you only stick to what you see and how you think people want you to act, you're going to be miserable even in a leadership role because you're not expressing yourself or giving your opinion. "These people don't just talk the talk, but they walk the walk. They lead by example in what might be the most impactful way possible— modeling. These true leaders do not expect others to do what they are not willing to do" (ASCD, 2018).

Effective leaders are often admired for the way they handle problems. Leaders aren't always people in management positions. You might find that one of your coworkers has leadership qualities that you admire. Sometimes management can have poor leaders, which often leads to turnover in jobs, which is why it is important to learn how to lead yourself. Develop the skills you need in order to be in control of your actions and know your capabilities when it comes to accomplishing your goals. You might find that you have to lead yourself in some scenarios as well. For example, you can teach yourself how to use new technology at work,   and then you will be able to teach others along the   way   when   they   are required to learn it for their positions as well.

 If you're going into a leadership position or aiming to be a leader one day, a question that will be asked during the interview is "What do you think you will contribute to this team?" Only you can answer that for yourself. People will have different answers and different expectations because we view situations differently. Your job as a leader is to convince them why you are right for the position and the good. Tell them the change you can bring to the team. You have gifts and talents for a reason. Use them. Be the leader that they didn't know they needed and enact the changes that big companies don't expect. Make your name by being different and making a difference, and you will see change happen right in front of you.

Be The Leader They Need

Being a leader and being responsible for your actions can mean brutal honesty that you don't want to hear. You have to be willing to let your ego go and realize that you are not better than the consequences that come with the actions you take. We have to learn from mistakes for a reason and be ready to just take charge again, picking up where we left off.

Being a leader and taking action isn't as easy as telling people what to do. Look at the way you communicate things to people. Are you commanding and forceful, or polite to the people listening? You don't want to be seen as the bad guy in a leadership position because it will make the job twice as had when people are not listening.

While you don't want to be demanding, it is important to be firm in your actions. In order for you to let things go and stay accountable, make a plan you are prepared to keep. Instead of saying, "We need to get people to sign up for the team," try saying, "Let's go get people signed up for the team today." Be firm in your convictions and expect success from yourself and your team. While you may not always get all the   way to the top of your standards, the positive   affirmation of success is likely to lead you there.

By setting your ego aside, a lot of the time it can clear up some of the confusion that clouds judgement. You want to build trust within coworkers to let them know that they can rely on you and expect competency and resilience from you when they are feeling down. Putting the thoughts away that you are above them or better than them and just being supportive and a part of the team will help you build that relationship with them.

When it comes to making team plans, prioritizing items and making strategies to execute the plan are what will help you be successful. When something goes wrong, fix it immediately. By allowing a problem to sit, you are opening the door to the possibility of other things going wrong. When one thing goes wrong, another is bound to follow and if you aren't quick at getting things resolved, problems will begin to snowball and you may begin to feel out of control.

If things begin to snowball: Stop. Take a step back and look at the entire picture without allowing yourself to get overwhelmed. Remember that you are in charge, you are responsible for you choices and at this moment, you have to make one effective enough to stop this impending   trouble. Once you have yourself   collected,   explain what needs to be done and why it needs to be done that way. Sometimes, people need a reason and explanation in order to process information that you give them. While this may seem like an unnecessary extra step, it can be beneficial to your team if it helps them be productive, which reflects positively on you.

When it comes to your display of emotion, it is important to stay positive throughout whatever is going wrong. A negative outlook will create a negative environment. If you are trying to get employees to power through a difficult day or a series of events gone wrong, negativity is going to drag you down even further. The emotional state of one person easily spreads, which is why you also should encourage positivity in the office everyday. Being a leader, it stands to reason that you will see other people's bad days while experiencing your own as well, and in order to not get stuck in that rut, you have to take responsibility for your feelings and thoughts and realize that if you are acting negatively, that will rub off on your team as well.

Leadership isn't for everybody and it can take some training to get you mind wrapped around the way to handle situations, but it's important you stay resilient and follow through with your plans and take responsibility for your actions in order to become the effective leader that you   are trying to be.

Another aspect of leadership and taking responsibility is being accountable for your employees' emotions when you think they are struggling. In order for a team to be successful and prosper together, everyone needs to be able to pull their weight in order to not bring others down or cause stress amongst the group. You should take time out of your day to check on people in the office and make sure that everyone is doing alright, or if they aren't, taking the time to sit with them and talk through some of the issues they are having.

Sincerity goes a long way on a team, and it also helps you to develop trust with one another, making your team stronger in the process. However you decide to go about it, building trust is essential to building a strong and willing team. Leaders often forget that their teams are the ones that are supporting them from below, and the struggles that they go through can cause morale to suffer if workers don't feel like a boss cares or has their interests in mind. "Everyone has vulnerabilities, emotions, and personality components for good or bad. By hiding those vulnerabilities, employees and managers are essentially denying a major part of their personalities. Vulnerability allows people to connect on a different level, which can lead to increased collaboration, productivity, and cohesiveness." (Morgan, 2017)

Chapter 6: Resilience

You've made it to the part of the journey where you can finally say you have successfully done it. You have pushed through different challenges and overcome the voices in your head telling you to quit. You were able to push through the hard parts of forming healthier habits, and you are starting to feel like you finally got something done.

But now isn't the time to relax. Even though it feels like your old behavior is long gone and that you have set yourself on a new trend, it's still easy to fall back into old patterns and let all your accomplishment go. It's time to be resilient in how you perform your task. It will start to feel a little tedious to go the extra mile every day when you feel like you have things under control. However, if you let those habits become relaxed, they could slip into the old ones, and you would be right back at square one.

You have to be resilient because you're still likely to mess up. You need to continuously reinforce the habits and skills that you've been working on. We've talked about mastering your craft in the last chapter. Remember that if you are going to stop practicing something, you will forget pieces of it over time. Sure, you would still know the basics, but you wouldn't really be a master anymore.

It takes a lot of patience and time before habits are completely set. They can easily change if there is a lifestyle change or new goals are being sought after. We also recently talked about what it means to be a leader. In most cases, we were talking about how to be a leader to others and be the best guide for them; however, you also have to be a leader for yourself.

You're the one in charge of your life. As you learn to adapt to your new life, your habits will as well. You will need to do whatever adjustment is needed to keep yourself in that right track. Keep yourself motivated. Once you've reached the top, you're not going to start climbing back down, are you? No. Keep building yourself up and working on new skills to keep yourself there. You get to the top by working hard, and you stay on top by working harder.

A part of resilience is having no fear of failure. The truth we often don't want to face is that we are likely to mess up a few times along the way. While it's frustrating and discouraging, being resilient is what is going to get you there in the end. Can you imagine if a baby stopped trying to walk after falling down a few times? It's a ridiculous thought because to us, a baby not walking sounds crazy. So why is it so easy to give up on going after your dreams when you fail?

Failure is your key to success. You're more than likely not going to get it right on the first try, and it's not expected that you would. As long as you are willing to try again and keep going, then you're not really failing. There are going to be forces working against you, sure, but when one strategy doesn't work, try a different one. Repeat this process until you succeed because that is all you can do to get it right. Failure isn't failure unless you stop trying. Continue to remind yourself what you are working for and what the goal you're trying to achieve is worth.

Your goals have to be the reason you get up in the morning and continue to work. They have to be the core of your dedication and the building blocks of your empire. You have to work for everything you have and don't expect anyone to give you handouts. More than likely, no one is going to hand you a bag of cash and say, "Go wild," because it's unrealistic. Don't expect things to be like that. Don't expect miracles to come along on the way to success because they won't. If they do, then you caught a very lucky break. Expect struggles. Expect failures. Expect to have to work twice as hard every time something doesn't work. Overcome every obstacle that gets in your way. Your power, your resilience, and your determination will keep you going when everything else seems not to be working.

Project 1 Is Done

Congratulations, you've made it through the hard part of accomplishing your first goal. You might be sitting there thinking that you haven't accomplished anything, but the truth of the matter is that you made it here. As you read this page, hopefully you've already taken steps to put your life back on track and become a better version of yourself. Accomplishing your first goal is a major step in the right direction as you work on forming new habits.

Some of the ways that you try to do to resolve different obstacles might not work. It is important that you learn from these ineffective ways and keep on trying to develop different techniques toward achieving your goal. It is okay to come across a few strategies that do not work for you in the beginning; eventually, you will have a better idea of how to get where you need to be in order to accomplish your goals.

Even if you haven't exactly perfected your habit-forming skills yet, go ahead and cross it off your to-do list as a reward to yourself. You have taken all the steps to put yourself on the correct path. Have your journal up to date and keep looking back at your goals, thinking, "What can I do next?"

One mistake this is often made when it comes to success is that people don't know what to do after they achieve it. While it isn't some grand mystery, it can be somewhat of a letdown after the first week or so of reaching that final destination of your goal. That's the reason you can't stop there. As you flip through your journal and review your goals, you will probably notice that some of them have in fact changed. Cross them off your list if they don't apply to your life anymore and move on.

You don't want to stop going after your other goals just because you reached one. The road doesn't end at the finish line; it's just the start of another race. You can take a break and enjoy the feeling that your progress has brought you because it is a huge accomplishment to be able to finish one of your goals; however, know that in a week or so, it's time to start back up and begin working on another one.

Think about it in terms of leadership for a moment. Once you reach management, are you going to stop trying to progress? No, you'd want to go higher, which means you would need to work harder to get there. With each goal, the difficulty of getting to the next level might increase, but you can't let that fear stop you. Instead, motivate yourself to keep going. You do not   stop thinking about the next step when you are sitting at the CEO desk and signing people's checks. The truth of the matter is that even if you are already a CEO, you still have to look for improvement and expansion because the idea of not making waves and halting progress isn't something in the plans.

We come back to the concept of mental toughness and the change that it will have on your life. Once you start making a change and feel the improvement in your life, you're not going to want to let that feeling go. So yes, the work might get tougher, but you just have to get tougher with it. Be resilient and be determined to succeed. Push past others. I think the best comparison when it comes to success is school graduation.

Think back to when you graduated from elementary school. You were thrilled to finally be a middle-school kid. When you graduated middle school, the same feeling applied to high school. Then when you finally graduated high school, you had the option to stop moving forward. If you didn't attend college, there is nothing wrong with that because you're still out there working hard and can still make your way to the top. College isn't for everyone, and there isn't anything wrong with not wanting to go to college.

However, if you did take the next educational step and push through the many years of college, you probably dealt with a lot of stressed-out nights and cramming sessions. You had to toughen yourself mentally to achieve your bigger goal. You went to college for something. You wanted to be someone with certain capabilities that others don't have. Can you remember the feeling of success when you graduated? If you haven't yet graduated, imagine it. It is a feeling to revel in and remember forever. That moment is the feeling of success. All the hard work and late-night frustrations led you to this moment of undeniable success and perfect completion.

Hold on to that feeling and think about every step along the way in the future. Whenever it feels like you are not going to break or that it just isn't worth the struggle anymore, recall that feeling. Recall that moment of relief and satisfaction in yourself when you pushed through and won the battle.

There are definitely going to be times when you feel discouraged. There will be times when the progress you're making isn't enough, or maybe you're not making any progress at all. You have to push those thoughts aside. Turn that negativity around and only focus your energies on what you can accomplish. Some projects are going to take more time, and some goals could take years and years of achieve, but that's why you have to keep pushing through your struggles.

You might come to a time in your life when you have to put your goals aside and help others around you, but don't let that be the end either. Sometimes when we put our personal wants and needs behind those of others, we forget that we actually need them. You can't let that be your end, though. If you need to take a break, then do so. If you need to help others for a little while, that's fine, but don't give up. Don't stop chasing those dreams and goals. Failure doesn't come from the lack of success, but it comes from the lack of trying again. Push through the problems and get back up. You made it here, and "here" is a big step and an accomplishment in itself. Keep that in mind and keep going.

You should celebrate your victories with your coworkers and employees along the way. By celebrating your success, it makes you more inclined to continue to do a good job. It falls into the same category as rewarding yourself for your success but this time, you should promote the positive feelings that are coming from the success of working together and accomplishing a project that had been difficult for the group. While it's easy to take a sigh of relief when big tasks are over, you have to remind yourself and your team that it's just a step on the ladder. Being a successful team doesn't come from finishing one project but instead comes from the willingness to push through all the projects and adapt to new strategies whenever you hit a hard point.

Finishing every project should be a relief for the team, but you should be able to encourage people to want to do more and strive to complete more than just the first project or just the basic needs. As a leader, your encouragement is vital to the success of a team. Your positive attitude and belief in the people you work with can make or break the team and, as a result, the success of the company.

Persuasion and Influence

To become successful, you need to be persuasive and influential. Influence often comes with time. Your reputation and the number of people that you know and made contact and connections with will affect the amount of influence you have over people.

The big question is how to be persuasive and how to get involved with people that will take you to the top. There are many ways to sway people, and I call this the external thought process. The external thought process is a little bit more than just observation and action. When it comes to persuasion, you need to make people think that they are in charge of the conversation.

Have you ever met someone who talks very slow or very fast? You match their speed because that's the environment they are creating. You want your audience to be on the same level as you. For example, if you're sitting in a conference room with a bunch of people in suits, more than likely you aren't going to be speaking quickly or in a higher pitch full of excitement. Instead, you'd slow your tempo so that everyone can hear you and clearly understand the point you are trying to get across. You'll probably even talk in a   lower voice than normal because it is soothing to others and brings comfort and resolution to the front of their thoughts.

On the other hand, if you are trying to persuade people, it would be great to get people's blood pumping. You're going to be moving faster and talking a little higher. It puts the mind on alert. Feed it with as much information as it can while it's excited and expectant of what could come next. Match your environment and bring a level of confidence to the table. Convince people that you're the right person that they should work with so that they will put their trust in you.

Another part of being persuasive is confidence. I think confidence can actually get you through a lot of challenging aspects of life. If people think that you are flustered or clueless, they will take advantage of that. Be a person who doesn't get stepped on. Be strong enough to hold your own beliefs.

A real-world example of this is in the retail environment. There are a lot of things you learn from working in customer service, and persuasion is definitely pretty high on the list. When you work in retail, your job is to sell someone something. However, selling something is the last thing you are going to do. First, you make friends with your customer and make them feel welcome. Then find out why they   are there and what it is they are looking for. Caring about people's personal life is important because it shows value in the relationship you're developing. Let's be honest here—you're going to buy something from your friend and from someone who cares about you. So show that you care. Learn about your customer.

What does that have to do with persuasion? Sell yourself to your audience well enough, and nothing will stop you. You might not have the expertise when it comes down to business meetings or introductions to new clients, and that's why you need to hone that art as fast as you can. After working for eight years in retail, I can elevator-pitch someone on nearly anything in less than a minute. You have to be personable and concise and sincere.

You will develop your own patterns over time and learn how to approach different situations well. As long as you can sell yourself, you can convince people of almost anything. Then there comes the influence. Once you have shown enough people that you know what you're talking about and how to go about handling different aspects of life, whether it be personal or in business, you will build a reputation. With reputation comes influence.

A perfect example of influence is the use of cleaning products. If you have been using Windex all your life and it has worked the entire time for everything you used it for, why would you stop using it? You wouldn't. When Windex releases a new line of products, like sponges, cleaning cloths, or even just a spray bottle, your mind clicks over to the success of those products because you know that Windex has never failed you. Sure, that sponge might cost more, but it was made by a company that you know has never failed in its ability to clean your house. Windex has that influence over you, and unknowingly, you are persuaded you to buy their other products because you know their reputation.

Influence comes from trust and being consistent. When you develop connections with people and they start to trust you, you will have influence over them. Just like persuasion, if people trust you and believe in you, they are more likely to believe what you say. So whether you are trying to sell someone something or influence their opinion on a certain aspect of a business, you have to create a bond with them. Show them that you are listening and that you care about what they have to say.

When a company decides to sign a contract with you, it signifies having a good relationship. For example, if your company signs a contract with Windex, their reputation will be transferred to your company as well. When you've built trust with a significant company, everyone who   trusts that company and knows   that   company   transfers   that   trust   to you by association. Build your reputation the right way and have the ability to be persuasive over people because it will be the next step to getting your foot in the door.

The language of persuasion often uses future tense in order to drive a point. By explaining that something *is* going to happen a certain way, you are putting certainty that it's going to happen in general. Set others into the mindset that they have to do things differently in order to create the outcome they are looking for.

If you have any doubts when you're trying to persuade someone into doing something, it is best to express your own opinions. If you aren't positive that something is going to work, admit that openly, but reassure and enforce the concept that you will get it figured out no matter what it takes. Don't let your influence suffer at the cost of being right. Admitting that you might not be 100 percent will show people that you are not trying to fool them. Build trust in your relationship with other people. Show them that while you may end up making an error along the way, you are going to fix it and solve the situation for them as your client.

Now that you have built yourself up to be a leader and have been placed in   charge of a team, what does that mean as far as   influence   and persuasion? Your team knows all the sweet talk and truth behind the sales tactics, so in order to influence them and be persuasive in that situation, you have to be more upfront and in your face with things.

Take for example a retail store trying to promote their in-store credit card. No one wants to open a credit card and more than likely, if they don't shop there often, it's going to be something they quickly shut down. So how do you keep the spirits of your employees up when they are constantly hearing "no"? The best solution I can offer right now is the idea that you make it fun. It's a lot of nonsense, but you're the one that's going to take the heat if your employees don't reach their quota. By making something like getting card members signed up into a competition, it builds competitiveness in the team and makes each member want to succeed that much more.

You also need to keep that positive attitude that you've been working on. If your team members think you have a negative attitude about a particular situation, they are going to hop on that train with you and be more unwilling to change their minds later on if they know you have dismissed it in your mind as well.

Model and Modify

Success will only last so long, though. With change comes new problems, and new problems require new solutions. This is where the model and modification come in. If you have a solution to a problem in the past, then why not use the same solution when faced with a similar situation?

The problem is when people try to use the same solution to solve a different problem. You have to adjust your solution to your problem. If you took your phone to a store and said that your phone wasn't working, you'd expect them to look at your phone and tell you what's wrong, such as the battery not holding a charge anymore. Then they would fix the problem, probably replacing the battery of the phone, and that would be that. But if you return a week later and say that it is still not working and they give you the same answer, would you be satisfied by that? No.

The idea of creating a model isn't to fit all the details of the problem but instead to begin the process of modification and solution. Think of a model house. The other houses built may look the same on the outside, but they have a few differences. On the inside, there might be three or four different floor plans. There is a model to start you off, and then there is the modification to narrow it down to the solution.

A modification was made by Coca-Cola to their product that made them stand out. Everyone in the world knows the polar bear Coca-Cola cans because it's a modification to a model that they already know is a success.

If you're wondering why you would even need to use a model in the first place, especially if you are going to modify it anyway, think about it like this: You wouldn't build a different style of house in the same neighborhood. You want things to look smooth and nice and like they belong there.

It's the same idea with any model. You don't need to start from scratch. One situation can be similar to thousands of other situations out there. Every problem will need its own fix, but like fixing a phone, step 1 is just identifying the problem, and step 2 is opening the issue up.

The process of change is just a big puzzle. Every piece has its place in the puzzle, but each one is connected to at least two others. In the case of model and modification, you have to learn to adapt to what needs to be done and corrected. You need to develop yourself and know the   things you are good at. Be able to make genuine   connections with people.

Mental toughness isn't a process on its own; it is a whole bunch of processes that are put together to create a fortitude of skills to help make your life easier and to bring you to a place where you can accomplish your goals and help others accomplish theirs.

Mental toughness has its own modifications as well. Not every piece of advice can be applied to every single person. You have to modify it to fit your life and the different aspects that you need to get through in order to be successful.

Some situations may call for the creation of an entirely new strategic model, especially if you have never faced a similar situation before. There will be times when you will have to work on something new and something that you have never dealt with before. Don't let this be something that stuns you or causes you distress. You just have to figure out a solution to the problem, and that will become the new model that you will be able to change and modify later on when you run into a problem similar to this.

New problems will constantly arise as situations change and new strategies develop, so it's important to stay prepared and be able to create new strategies for situations that haven't been dealt with. You have to be capable of making those changes and accepting those changes to stay productive, and you have to keep your calm when stressful situations arise.

The model and modify tactic also comes into play when you look at people in the workplace. When acting as a leader, you could have to deal with some tension between employees from time to time. Most situations are likely to work themselves out, but you can always guide people in the right direction if it seems like they need it.

The basic model of relationships stand on respecting one another, and if you're dealing with coworkers that can barely tolerate each other, there is more than likely a problem having to do with respect. While employees don't have to be the best of friends, they do need to respect each other and maintain a level of tolerance for one another while working on the same team. With that being said, sometimes you have to modify the model for business relationships in order for people to get along. Most of the time, having a sit down conversation with both parties can help resolve underlying issues between people, but if that doesn't work, you might have to search through different techniques and problem solving strategies to maintain the peace on your team.

You are responsible for your decisions and the actions of your team, which is the reason you need to keep everyone on the same page about how to respect one another and why it is mandatory on the team. There will be challenges you face internally and externally, and while you're working on the internal mental toughness process and making yourself better, you still have to be supporting your team and encouraging them as they deal with their internal issues and external work issues.

The relationship model can be applied to customer relations as well. You could be dealing with agitated customers which can lead to frustrated employees and, again, negative energy being released while you're trying to be positive.

You have to remember that while you're dealing with internal problems and external problems, so is everyone else. Those people are also looking to you for answers and guidance for when things go wrong and might ask for your help if they don't think they are able to work through the issues alone. As a leader, you have to be prepared to take on that stress and be there for your peers at work or family and friends at home that trust you to be there. There is a lot going on all at once and while we talk about how to handle the mental stress, it's another thing to be able to take that advice and actually make it happen.

While you're trying to help others, always remember that you're still your first priority.

The model to base everything off of is your happiness and your success. If you don't have yourself under control, you will be in no position to help others solve their problems or lead a group of people that are counting on you. Model yourself after who you want to be and develop your character, then help others get there.

Chapter 7: Summing Up Mental Toughness

The reason you're here is to reset your life and begin yourself on a better path. Through this book, you have learned about the different steps to achieve mental toughness. However, you haven't exactly learned the key elements to it.

One element rarely discussed when it comes to mental toughness is the fact that when times get tough, you don't get to complain about it. Complaining creates negative thoughts, and it turns all your hard work against you. It takes a lot of energy to complain, and you could use that energy to try to solve your problem and move on instead. Complaining isn't going to get you anywhere. Even though it doesn't seem to affect you, in the long run, it will affect the way your brain is processing information. Complaining undermines mental toughness and fortitude.

Whining isn't going to help you change the events that have happened either. We talked previously about the ability to let go of things that are out of your control. It is useless to argue with people and try to make them understand something if they are not willing to listen. No matter how hard you try or how much energy and effort you put into it, you're not going to be able to change their minds.

One of the keys to mental toughness is being in control of your emotions. Even during times when you feel down, you still have to pretend that you have it together. Remember the idea that if you keep smiling, you'll be happier? The same concept applies here. If you act like you have no idea what you're doing and you're frazzled and lost, your brain will send those signals to your body. If you can convince your brain, though, that you do have it under control and that you know what you're doing even when you don't, it will limit that urge of panic. You will be able to think more clearly and have an easier time keeping your mind where it needs to be focused.

Mental toughness is all about what you are willing to do for yourself. If you don't believe in yourself, you aren't going to end up feeling successful. If you are trying to change for someone else, you are going to have a harder time than normal because you aren't changing for yourself. You don't need to impress others. You have to fight the urge to do so when your brain sends out that signal. What other people think of you does not affect the actual person that you are, and you certainly shouldn't let it. Have the mental fortitude to push those thoughts and needs to satisfy others because they aren't important enough for you to concentrate on.

Behind Mental Toughness

It's easy to give up, especially when the going gets tough and your goals don't feel worth it anymore. You have to have the willpower to continue though. "Willpower can be thought of as a combination of intention, effort and courage" (Seeman, 2018). Gary Seeman has a PhD in psychology, and he goes on to talk about the different aspects of willpower in great detail. He says that intention is pretty much the "will" in "willpower." You have to want it more than anything else in order for this to work. You have to stay on task and force yourself through your activities in order to be successful at the end of the day.

Willpower is the push that people often talk about when they want to start a new goal or when they are working on achieving something in life. Typically, people want reassurance coming from other people that they won't fail and that they can do it. However, you also need to have self-belief. If someone tells you that you are a great dog   sitter   and   that   dogs absolutely love you, that   is a great boost to your confidence. However, it isn't going to help you much if you're afraid of dogs. You obviously will not have the willpower to keep taking care of animals if you don't like being in their presence. People can tell you that are good at something, but you'll also have to find it in yourself to believe that.

Then there is effort. Effort is how much energy you put into something. If you don't want it, you won't do it. Willpower is the push that keeps you going, but effort is what you're putting in. Another way to think of effort is how much time you work toward something. If you decide to learn to paint, but you only practice once a week, then you aren't putting in a ton of effort to learn that skill. If it's something you are thrilled to do and you are excited about learning, then you'd probably put in a lot of effort by practicing every day and working on perfecting different techniques. The amount of effort that you put in is the amount of success you will get back. Don't expect to be an expert of something if you never work to get better at it. You can compare effort to calligraphy. Being able to write smoothly in the script takes a very long time and a lot of patience. You have to practice it over and over to keep the steadiness and overall ability intact.

Lastly, there is courage. Mental toughness takes a lot of courage, and this could be one of the most challenging parts. When doubts and fears take over, it can be extremely difficult to push those thoughts aside and focus on the positive. Earlier in the book, we discussed how to overcome those anxious feelings and how to calm yourself. However, you also have to summon courage within yourself to overcome those fears. You have to be brave when you fail and be willing to try again even if it seems that all the odds are stacked against you at that point. Successful people just push through and refuse to give up when times are tough.

Mental toughness can also be defined as "the ability to execute at a peak level of performance in all situations without getting distracted and with complete mental clarity and ease. Some call this being in the zone" (Walker, 2018). If you think about it in the sense of being in the zone, then it might be a little bit clearer for you to proceed. Being in the zone is when you are so focused on what you're doing that everything else around you completely disappears. Sometimes when you're in the zone of total concentration, you might not even realize what time it is.

"Staying mentally tough will not only give us the strength we need to deal with our mistakes or sub-par performance, but also provide us with the resilience to keep going despite them. When events don't go our way (or the way we expect), we cannot lose focus or determination. By the very definition of mental toughness, we must continue to persevere through the adversities with which we are faced" (Fader, 2018).

A great way to keep yourself on track when trying to be mentally tough is to talk to yourself before you begin working. Self-talk enables you to coach yourself and motivate before you begin working toward your goals. It certainly wouldn't hurt to give yourself a small self-talk every day. It will keep you inspired and hyped up about your life and the different activities you are going to be working on. It could be something as simple as "You can do this, and you're going to do your best. You are going to be successful at work today and not let anything get you down." But you still have to hold yourself accountable to that statement as well.

Mental toughness is a blend of everything, but a lot of it comes down to holding yourself accountable and expecting more out of yourself than anyone else. Be responsible for your actions and show people that you are worthy of success. If you want that promotion, then work as hard as you can for it. Show your boss that you are the best person for the job because you can do the job better than anyone else. People might talk bad about you or say you're showing off. That's okay. Show off your talents and your capabilities and let   other people take notice. Don't let their jealousy   get   you   down,   but instead, let it inspire you to work harder.

It's important to remain flexible and take everything in stride. Just like when you modify a model to fit your needs in a new scenario, you have to be flexible with your life. Be accepting of the change that is ultimately going to be pushed onto you as you become more organized and prepared. Being flexible will also help you to stress less about the events happening around you. If you are willing to go with the flow and let things change as they need to, you'll notice that you won't feel quite as worried about getting things done.

One aspect often forgotten about in mental toughness is being supportive of others along their journey as well. Just because you are having a hard time doesn't mean you should bring others down with any negativity. You wouldn't want anyone to push negativity onto you when you are striving to be successful. By motivating and supporting others, you will feel more positive and resilient yourself. Mental toughness is supporting yourself and others toward the process of change.

It is easy to forget about other people, especially when you are having a tough time yourself. When you are so focused on changing or improving something in your life, you may not notice that you are hurting other people along the way.

It's important that in mental toughness you don't become oblivious to your other emotions and you do allow yourself to be vulnerable at times in order to deal with those emotions when they arise. You have to remember that you are putting a lot of pressure on yourself, as your goal is to be a better version of you. Don't feel like you have to cram all of your emotions into a small box when you start feeling sad or frustrated. Expressing those emotions and dealing with the external events of your life takes just as much out of you mentally as other aspects that you are fighting with in your mind. Give yourself a break every now and then to rest and recuperate before beginning on the path again.

Activating Your Inner CEO

My last advice for you to achieve mental toughness and live your best life is to be the CEO of yourself every day. People are going to try to tear you down. You can't let that be the case. Your best life will only be achieved once you're happy with yourself. It doesn't matter what stage of life you are at. People are constantly going to try to tear you down and lower your self-worth. You have to summon your inner strength and call upon your inner CEO.

Sometimes to be your best self, you have to get over what other people have to say about you. If a person gets on your nerves and simply doesn't respect the boundaries you try to set with them, you can always take it up with a superior. A former boss of mine told me something that has stuck through the years, and I have taken it with me to every job I have had. She said, "If someone is deliberately pushing you down and you continue to stand back up, you win. They will continue to bother you as long as you seem bothered. If you can sit there and smile through it, they will get bored."

People will talk until you shut them down. It takes a bit of confidence, but don't allow yourself to be stepped on. If someone is talking badly about you or trying to put you down instead of celebrating successes with you, ask them to leave. There is nothing wrong with telling someone that their negativity doesn't need to be a part of your life. As the CEO of your life, treat it like a business. If someone doesn't fit, don't force them. It's a hard lesson to learn, but those who make your life hard need not be a part of it anymore. If you continue to welcome people who are working to bring you down, you're going to end up stacking challenges against yourself.

Be the boss of your life and respect yourself to know when enough is enough. You can call the shots and know what hurts you and what helps you. If you have best friends lifting your spirits and cheering you on, then of course, you want to include them in your life and your goals. They will help keep you motivated when you feel down. But those who are negative aren't going to change. They don't want to change. You need to fire them from your life and don't look back.

For a second, imagine that you run your own company but you don't want to get up early in the morning. Even if you don't want to, you still have to, right? Your job is to be in charge of the company and make sure that everything is running smoothly. You don't want anything to go off the rails while you're   off   slacking   somewhere else. Being the boss means that you have to keep everything and everyone in check, including yourself.

They always say to dress to impress when you go to an interview or an important meeting, but really, dress to impress every day even if it is only just for yourself. If you look good, you're likely to feel more confident and project that feeling as well. People are drawn to those who seem more exuberant. It's the same thing with being persuasive and having influence over others. You aren't going to want to work for a company that isn't energetic or excited to have you there, but rather, you want to be part of a company where people are smiling and having a good time.

Make sure you appreciate yourself. By giving yourself value, you boost your own self-esteem, and you can create a happier feeling. People stay where they feel appreciated and feel wanted. If you don't want to be there yourself and you don't feel confident in your ability to stay positive when things go wrong, then focus on improving your own perceptions. Even though some people don't need to be in your life, you still might have to interact with them. If you're in the office space with someone who rubs you the wrong way, you still have to work with them. It's unfortunate, but you still have to make the best out of that situation. Keep up your positive attitude despite having to work with people you don't necessarily like.

Another part of channeling your inner CEO is accepting the things that you can't change. Unfortunately, unless you are the boss, you are not able to fire anyone yet, so you have to learn to manage how to feel around them. It comes back around to focus and deciding not to let different things bother you. Don't let outside factors, like other people or unchangeable situations, create self-doubt. Be your own person and stand your ground when it comes to situations like that. Mental toughness isn't just applied to goals and tasks. Control yourself and have control of your life.

There will be times that are tougher than others. Sometimes quitting seems a lot easier than pushing through to the end, but being the CEO of your life lets you know that that is not an option. You worked hard to get here, and you'll have to work just as hard to stay here. Make living your life and feeling successful a priority because at the end of the day, focusing on your progress and your goal is all that you can do. CEOs of big companies do not worry about people talking badly about them because they are already at the top. Focus on improving yourself and building your mental toughness in order to be the best version of yourself.

Mental toughness is something you are going

to have to practice and work on constantly. Keep yourself mentally up to date and willfully strong. If you want to be successful and feel successful, then take control of your life. Stop accepting anything less than the standard you set for yourself and demand that level from yourself.

As you begin making important choices for your life, you should think about the future you are developing as well. It's similar to the idea that you shouldn't burn a bridge you have to walk across. It's important to take responsibility for your actions when you make them as well, because in the future if it does affect something negatively, you need to be able to stand up and help solve the problem it caused.

While most people don't think about the effects of future decisions when it comes to decision making, you should try and make it a priority to think ahead and problem solve in advance.

It is easy enough to blame someone else when things go wrong, especially if it's after the decision you made. Passing off blame is human, but not responsible. Think, for example, of a mundane excuse: I didn't have time.

If you were asked to go out and buy some chicken to cook for dinner, then you need to be accountable for that. However, if you "don't have time" and don't bring chicken home, someone else is probably going to get the blame for dinner not getting done on time. So, would you allow the blame for a late dinner to be on someone else? Or would you stand up and say it was your fault for not getting the chicken home on time?

When it comes to responsibility and being accountable for your actions and the results of your future actions, you do have to think ahead and be prepared for when things fall back on you. It is a big part of mental toughness, but it's also ownership and doing the right thing by you and others in life.

Taking ownership of your actions comes with being a leader as well. You are responsible for yourself and others. Their actions reflect on your behavior as their leader and you will be held responsible for their actions as well because you are in charge of overseeing them.

Another thing for you to consider as you embrace your inner CEO is that everyone may not like you. Try as you might, some people cannot be pleased and you're just going to have to deal with that as it comes. There is a difference in being a leader and being a manager. A manager is someone who manages. They might not necessarily be the friendliest supervisor you have ever had and could probably learn a thing or   two about how to guide people on how to get   tasks accomplished. But their job is paperwork and managing how things get accomplished and turned over to whoever is next in line, whereas being a leader is pretty different. Leaders don't necessarily manage people. Sometimes they are just team members that others look to for advice or guidance.

In more and more big businesses, you will see managers assigning team lead roles to certain individuals, and while they don't have as much power as a manager, if any more than a regular team member, people on that team know that they can go to that person for help should they need it during the work day. Being a CEO of your life is similar to business. Your brain is your team lead and your organs are in charge of getting things done in order to keep you alive, and you need to build a cohesive team like that in order to keep things moving steadily through business. Have the brains of the group, it could even be you, passing down the message and the plan, and then let it go so your workers can get it done. If they can't get it done, it's time to replace them and move on. The shortest straw in the pack is still going to weigh it down and cause problems on the team.

Thanks!

Conclusion

Talking about mental toughness, you have to prepare yourself to face struggles, anxiety, depression, and self-doubt along the way. It's easy enough for people to pass mental toughness as the idea that you just have to push through some hard times. However, it isn't that easy.

Through this book, you have learned how to handle stress and anxiety that can come with setting new goals. You have also learned how to go about setting up a journal that is going to help you accomplish your goals. Mental toughness starts at the base, and you may have to make modifications along the way that will fit you and your personality for you to be successful.

More than anything else, mental toughness is about finding the strength within yourself. It isn't about how many goals you've accomplished in a year or how much money you make. While those things can measure success, mental toughness is something you have to measure on your own. You can't necessarily compare yourself to anyone else because their willpower and yours are completely different, and with different lifestyles come different responsibilities and capabilities.

In the future, you may come across harder goals to accomplish, or you might start to feel like things are falling apart again. It's okay when that happens; it is easy for things to get out of control. If you continue to practice mental toughness, you will have a better chance of putting the pieces back in place when they begin to get chaotic. Sometimes, you might just need to step back and redo your schedule or reorganize your journal. Every six months, do a refresh on your plans and make sure you're still on track. It also keeps you aware of what you still have left of your goals to accomplish.

I hope that through this book, you have learned how to be your strongest. In the twenty-one days that this book has set you up for as much success as you are willing to accomplish, there will be times when success seems too far. Sometimes giving up seems like a good idea. Hopefully, you'll return to your journal and remind yourself of all the goals you've set. Remember your successes and where your mistakes took you. Look at all the history you've made. If you're only at day 22 in building a habit, remember that change takes a lot of time. Power through the struggle.

You might have to reset your life a few times before you get things right, and that's okay. Life isn't anywhere near perfect, and you might hit a few brick walls along the way to your best life.

Don't let those mistakes derail your positivity. If you couldn't do it, you wouldn't have made it this far. If you didn't believe you could be successful, you wouldn't be reading this sentence at the end of the book.

Be the leader you would want to have, and set high expectations for yourself in order to better yourself and the team you are developing in the workplace. If you don't believe in your own success, how could you expect someone else to? Recognize that your life is far from perfect and demand a better tomorrow out of yourself, especially when times seem tough. By forcing yourself to continue through the hard times and keep positivity high in the workspace, you are leading your team effectively.

Success is something that does come from within, and while it takes a lot of work and typically a lot of time, it's worth it. The feeling at graduation and the emotional relief when something works out—those feelings will stick with you and will make you feel successful when the hard times come. Don't be afraid of the future. You've got this. You have all the tools for success. You just have to choose to use them the best you can.

References

Action for Happiness (2017, June 17). Action 16: Setting goals. Retrieved from https://www.actionforhappiness.org/take-action/set-your-goals-and-make-them-happen

ASCD (2017, March 16). What it means to be a true leader. Retrieved from http://inservice.ascd.org/what-it-means-to-be-a-true-leader/

Clear, J. (2018, July 30). How positive thinking builds skills, boosts health, and improves work. Retrieved from https://jamesclear.com/positive-thinking

Fader, J. (2018, October 03). What Is mental toughness? Retrieved from https://jonathanfader.com/mental-toughness/

Faustino, A. (2017, August 16). Unlock your potential: 3 keys to harnessing your hidden aptitudes. Retrieved from https://www.goalcast.com/2017/08/16/unlock-potential-3-keys-harnessing-hidden-aptitudes/

Haden, J. (2014, July 23). 7 Habits of people with remarkable mental toughness. Retrieved from https://www.inc.com/jeff-haden/7-habits-of-people-with-remarkable-mental-toughness.html

Kutcher, J. (2017, December 08). Harnessing your skills to craft your dream job. Retrieved from https://jennakutcherblog.com/106/

Mayo Clinic Staff. (2017, February 18). How to stop negative self-talk. Retrieved from https://www.mayoclinic.org/healthy-lifestyle/stress-management/in-depth/positive-thinking/art-20043950

Riordan, Christine M. Six elements of mental toughness. *Forbes*, 11 July 2012, www.forbes.com/2010/09/17/executive-mental-toughness-leadership-managing-athletes.html#24cbcf1c2101.

Seeman, G. (2018, October 08). The psychology of mental toughness. Retrieved from https://psychcentral.com/lib/the-psychology-of-mental-toughness/

Selk, J. (2013, April 16). Habit formation: The 21-day myth. Retrieved from https://www.forbes.com/sites/jasonselk/2013/04/15/habit-formation-the-21-day-myth/#4e1e22eddebc

Sly, S. (2017, August 02). Why mental toughness is important to your success in life, Health, and Wealth. Retrieved from https://susansly.com/why-mental-toughness-is-important-to-your-success-in-life-health-and-wealth/

Sparks, D. (2018, January 31). Home remedies: Anxiety and stress. Retrieved from https://newsnetwork.mayoclinic.org/discussion/home-remedies-anxiety-and-stress/

Walker, A. (2018, April 04). What is mental toughness? Retrieved from http://www.mentaltoughnessinc.com/what-is-mental-toughness/